Personal Training

Active Learning in Sport – titles in the series

Coaching Science	ISBN 978 1 84445 165 4
Personal Training	ISBN 978 1 84445 163 0
Researching Sport and Exercise	ISBN 978 1 84445 164 7
Sport Sociology	ISBN 978 1 84445 166 1

To order, please contact our distributor: BEBC Distribution, Albion Close, Parkstone, Poole, BH12 3LL. Telephone: 0845 230 9000, email: learningmatters@bebc.co.uk. You can also find more information on each of these titles and our other learning resources at www.learningmatters.co.uk

Personal Training

Mark Ansell

LearningMatters

To Jenni and Rheya

First published in 2008 by Learning Matters Ltd

British Library Cataloguing in Publication Data
A CIP record for this book is available from the British Library

ISBN: 978 1 84445 163 0

Cover and text design by Toucan Design
Project Management by Diana Chambers
Typeset by Kelly Gray
Printed and bound in Great Britain by TJ International Ltd, Padstow, Cornwall

Learning Matters Ltd
33 Southernhay East
Exeter EX1 1NX
Tel: 01392 215560
E-mail: info@learningmatters.co.uk
www.learningmatters.co.uk

FSC
Mixed Sources
Product group from well-managed
forests and other controlled sources
Cert no. SGS-COC-2482
www.fsc.org
© 1996 Forest Stewardship Council

Contents

Acknowledgements

I would like to thank my work colleagues at City and Islington College in London: Alex, Elena, Mark, Claire, Andrew and Preya for their support and advice. I would also like to thank my previous students Daryl and Davinia for the modelling in the exercise library section. Thank you also to Shelley for the help with the manual resistance section.

Foreword

Personal training is fast becoming one of the most popular career choices, with its scope for flexible work hours, vast potential for earnings and its relaxed, fulfilling and enjoyable work environment. The industry has become flooded with texts and courses, all promoted as being the best in their area. However, no book in the UK has tried to cover all the most important fundamentals of personal training.

Personal Training achieves this, doing so within an easy-to-follow structure. This book covers in depth the main areas a personal trainer would need to know. Written by Mark Ansell, a highly regarded lecturer and personal trainer, it takes into account both his vast experience and research, making it a must-have for any would-be personal trainers, undergraduate and foundation degree students and current personal trainers.

This is an ideal book for anyone studying or working in personal training, particularly from a UK perspective, as there appears to be some confusion as to what makes a 'personal trainer' in the UK. This book helps resolve this and sets out an excellent base for up-and-coming personal trainers, helping to provide an exemplary reference for anyone in, or looking to get into, the fitness industry.

Having worked and lectured in the industry for the last seven years, I know first hand what an important tool this text will provide for anyone interested in personal training.

Jon Brazier, BA, CSCS

PART 1

Foundations

Chapter 1

Personal training

The number of books devoted to personal training is growing. Most of the current textbooks have been written and published in the US. Few have been written and published specifically for readers in the UK. While the American books can certainly help with scientific aspects of personal training, little information on personal training in the UK is available in textbooks. This book aims to fill the gap. It is aimed at students on UK fitness-related degree courses, prospective personal trainers (PTs) and those already employed, and anyone else with an interest in personal training.

Personal training in the UK has evolved from the traditional gym instructor role that developed in the early 1980s. The UK has followed the US model for personal training that developed with the assistance of the National Strength and Conditioning Association (NSCA) and the American College of Sports Medicine (ACSM). These organisations have striven to make personal training a professional career path for trainers. It is fortunate that their qualifications are available in the UK, along with those of other UK-based training providers who have recognised the need for different levels of fitness certification. Universities and colleges in the UK offer some excellent sport and exercise degree courses that cover the science of training to a level that no private training organisation could hope to do and these provide the best route for prospective trainers' career development. Now there are foundation degrees that offer work-based learning as part of the study experience. These courses encourage students to earn while they learn. This is a fairly new model for degree learning in the UK and is catching on fast. However, all degree students will still need to gain industry qualifications in addition in order to work in the profession.

In the UK trainers will usually start out with a level 2 gym instructor award, which allows them to perform client inductions, programming and more general gym duties such as floor walking. (The 'Starting in the industry' section in Chapter 12 gives further detail on level 2 qualifications.) Gym instructors often soon realise that personal training work provides opportunities for enhanced status and income. Most gym instructors will move on to a qualification that will allow them to join the Register of Exercise Professionals (REPs) as a level 3 PT. Entry on the register shows that the trainer has a recognised qualification and has demonstrated the basic knowledge needed to operate as a personal trainer in gyms in the UK. This does not mean, however, that a PT *must* complete only REPs-registered courses to practise as a personal trainer in the UK. Some, but by no means all, gyms in the UK require PTs to be level 3 REPs. Bizarrely, REPs does not currently recognise many American qualifications that are at least equal to UK counterparts. To ensure compliance with REPs requirements, trainers and prospective trainers will need to search the list of recognised qualifications on the REPs website (**www.exerciseregister.org**). For a trainer moving into self-employment and home training, or working in a gym that does not stipulate level 3 REPs, however, the American NCSA, ACSM or ACE qualifications may be more applicable.

If you are interested in becoming a PT, you will want to find out exactly what PTs do and what roles they fulfil. The role of the personal trainer can be diverse. Working as a PT you will have to motivate your clients to achieve their fitness goals. In some cases you will have to act as a role model for healthy lifestyle choices to be made by your clients. You will be responsible for their well being while you are training them. You'll need to perform health screens and fitness tests, keep up-to-date records on all your clients, provide optimum training programmes, teach exercise techniques, be positive at all times, be flexible with your working hours, empathise with your clients, and be passionate about personal training! The job of PT requires many skills. It can, however, be extremely rewarding, especially when clients meet their goals.

As a PT, you will need an in-depth knowledge of how scientific understanding can be applied to everything you do in personal training. This book is designed to help by focusing on the *application* of knowledge. The hope is that you will develop your scientific knowledge of fitness and exercise alongside your business acumen. This provides the best chance of succeeding in the industry. Within the personal training sector there are the good trainers, the not-so-good trainers and a few downright dangerous trainers! Strive to be an *exceptional* trainer, using scientifically sound practice and always acting in a professional manner. This will give you an advantage over trainers who think that good is good enough.

This textbook has been designed to introduce readers to the science behind personal training and to explore it further. It is also designed to help them build successful careers whether working in gyms ('in-house') or in self-employment. It shows the need for synergy between the disciplines that PTs will encounter during their professional career. It is important to remember that personal training uses an holistic approach – that is to say, it requires the trainer to bring together understanding drawn from several disciplines. In one way or another, therefore, all the chapters in this book are linked.

It is hoped that you will keep this book handy to use as an essential reference text. Each chapter encourages readers to explore topics in greater detail by providing suggestions for further study. It is recommended that you keep a workbook to accompany your reading of this text. This will build into a further resource for you to use during your study. The information entered in your workbook will be driven mainly by the learning activities within each chapter.

Two features of the text have been designed to guide you throughout. These are:

- reflection boxes – these focus on the *application* of knowledge and draw on the author's own career experience to do so;
- activity boxes – these provide tasks for you to learn from. By attempting these you will learn by doing work that is linked to that chapter. One of the best ways

of learning is to produce your own mini assignments from these boxes. It is highly recommended that you develop the assignments most applicable to you into full-length reports. These reports will help you to decide which area of personal training you wish to pursue further.

Further reading

At the end of each chapter you will find a list of books and websites that will help you to explore further the topic covered by the chapter. If you were to buy one other textbook in addition to this one, I would recommend the NSCA's *Essentials of strength and conditioning*. The book can seem daunting for students new to personal training, but it does indeed cover *essentials* and it will lead you into further study.

Many helpful electronic resources consist of general personal training websites that cover a wide range of topics: some of the most useful are shown below.

www.ptonthenet.com – this is a subscription website that contains an excellent article section along with a huge exercise library; well worth visiting.

www.personaltraining1st.com – this site contains further information based on the chapters in this book. There is also a forum to join and downloads such as record forms used in this book.

www.exerciseregister.org – the Register of Exercise Professionals of the United Kingdom.

www.nsca-lift.org – the National Strength and Conditioning Association main site gateway.

www.acsm.org – the American College of Sports Medicine main site gateway.

www.acefitness.org – American Council on Exercise main site gateway.

www.leisureopportunities.co.uk – this site has lists of training providers for all levels of fitness qualifications in the UK.

www.ncbi.nlm.nih.gov/sites/entrez/ – the journal search engine that allows you to explore journal abstracts.

www.personaltrainertoday.com – a website that includes articles for PTs.

www.sponet.de – click on the British flag to gain entry to a search engine for sports journal articles.

www.pponline.co.uk – *Peak Performance* online gives access to a wealth of training information.

www.physsportsmed.com/ – complete journal articles are available from this website.

www.sportsci.org – lots of sport science articles can be found here.

www.sports-fitness-advisor.com – much information is available here on a variety of sport subjects.

Chapter 2

Programming essentials

This chapter explains how to produce training programmes. Programming forms the basis for training plans for all clients. A PT has to understand and apply the science behind programming in order to optimise clients' physical adaptation. Programming is central to a PT's daily work. If a PT were to train a client without the use of programming, then it is difficult to comprehend why they would be training the client at all! Programming provides PTs with a way of controlling upcoming sessions in order to ensure that clients make progress. The following topics in particular will be covered.

Foundations:

- training principles;
- programming building blocks: key terms;
- client needs analysis;
- exercise selection;
- exercise order;
- frequency and volume;
- avoiding overtraining.

Approaches:

- cardiovascular training modes;
- methods of resistance training;
- free weights versus machines;
- functional training.

Using programming tools:

- intensity guidelines;
- repetition ranges;
- sets;
- muscle balance;
- flexibility.

The chapter is designed to help you to:

1. understand the need for a scientific basis for exercise programming;
2. begin to produce professional programmes for personal training sessions;
3. explore topics further using other resources.

Introduction to programming

Long gone are the days when personal trainers could base training on hearsay and fads. Personal trainers today must strive to use scientific training methods wherever possible. They can benefit from the many years of exercise science research that have been undertaken. Though science rarely provides absolute proof of the effects of training methods, there is a wealth of empirical evidence that can be used to inform practice. Professional organisations such as REPs, the ACSM, NSCA and YMCA (a major provider of training for the UK fitness industry) all reinforce the need to be aware of using enlightened programming methods when training clients.

It is important to recognise that clients will come to a PT with many different goals. A great number will want to lose weight and make aesthetic gains. They may desire health benefits, to increase their flexibility, or become stronger. There will also be sport-specific clients wanting to improve their performance through the use of fitness training.

Foundations

Principles of training

All programming is based on one negative and three positive principles. They are:

*   reversibility (the negative principle) – 'if you do not use it, you lose it', that is, physiological systems will revert to a pre-trained state if a client stops training;
*   specificity – all physical training should be specific to the training goals of the client;
*   overload – physiology requires an overload of the system in order to adapt;
*   progression – all overload should be progressive in order to elicit optimum gains.

All of these principles relate to Hans Selye's general adaptation syndrome (GAS). Selye conducted pioneering research into the body's reaction to stressors. GAS incorporates these phases:

1. the *alarm phase* – the body's initial response to overload ;
2. the *resistance phase* – this is where adaptation occurs (generally post-training);
3. the *exhaustion phase* – where the body cannot cope with acute or chronic overload (and so physical work is compromised).

Figure 2.1: Aspects of Selye's general adaptation syndrome

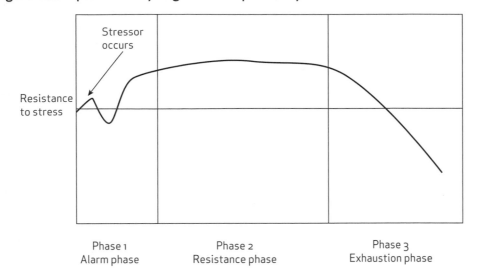

The alarm phase is directly related to the overload and specificity principles: a PT uses a specific training stimulus (e.g. cardiovascular or weight training) to overload the client's physiology. Progression is built in by the PT to increase the adaptation in the physiological system being trained – in effect manipulating the resistance phase. Progression is incorporated by altering the exercise variables (for example, the load borne in a weight-training exercise). The exhaustion phase should be avoided by PTs as this can lead to overtraining by the client and performance will actually decrease. Without the instigation of the alarm phase the human body will start to reverse the changes that have occurred (if a client stops training).

These principles are the cornerstones of every training session. Here is an example of the various phases in practice. A client performs a heavy weight-training session on a Monday that includes barbell chest press. During this workout the pectoral, tricep and anterior deltoid muscles experience the alarm phase, increasing the activation of the central nervous system (CNS). During the next 24–48 hours the body experiences the resistance phase: it adapts to the overload by remodelling the muscle tissue accordingly. This leads to an increased work output. Note that if the client were to train on the Tuesday for an extended period of time, the adaptation would reverse due to inadequate recovery time, leading to exhaustion.

Muscle contractions

The following types of muscle contraction will be mentioned in this chapter.

- Isometric: where the muscle contracts without movement (e.g. a three-quarter press-up held in position by the client).
- Isotonic: concentric (muscle-shortening) and eccentric (muscle-lengthening) contractions. For example, a barbell bicep curl (illustrated on page 100) employs both contractions of the bicep brachii muscle. Isotonic contractions are the most common type of muscle contraction in physical training.

- Isokinetic: the muscle keeps a constant velocity during contraction. This is usually achieved using specific equipment and is not therefore commonly used by personal trainers. The nearest example without equipment would be a muscle contracting underwater – the water provides a constant resistance velocity through the whole range of movement.

Programming building blocks: key terms

The two main forms of training are **cardiovascular (CV)** training and **resistance** training.

CV programming involves using modes of activity to work the heart and vascular systems, and is used to develop cardiovascular fitness. This is important both for helping clients perform day-to-day tasks and to increase their 'aerobic' fitness overall. The term 'cardiovascular endurance' can also be used to describe this component of fitness.

Resistance training programmes use weights (providing the load) to develop power, strength, muscle size (hypertrophy) or local muscular endurance (local effects are specific to the muscles worked in a particular activity). If the client's primary aim is improved general fitness, the best programmes will tend to use a mixture of CV and muscular endurance resistance training.

Each client comes with a **resistance training status.** This is dependent on the client's training history. For example, if the client has trained for more than one year they could be termed an advanced exerciser. The resistance training status will indicate whether the client is capable of more advanced training techniques such as power exercises.

The building blocks of resistance training are **repetitions (reps)** and **sets.** A single rep is an exercise performed once. A group of reps is called a set. Questions of rep ranges, set numbers and rest periods have all been researched scientifically in order to provide guidance on the best ways to achieve clients' goals.

Other important considerations include the rest periods between sets and also between sessions. We refer here to **frequency of training**. This is usually discussed relative to one-week blocks. For example, a client may train three times per week – on, say, a Monday, Wednesday and Friday – a frequency of three.

The **time** it takes the client **to perform one rep** helps to determine the ultimate muscular adaptation. Power exercises have a speed component and will therefore be executed faster than training for hypertrophy. The general guideline is that each rep should not be rushed and should take around four or five seconds in isotonic contractions. Remember that the client should be controlling the resistance in the eccentric phase (not just letting drop!).

Muscle balance (described below) concerns the client's healthy balance of muscle on all sides of their body. If a client exhibits muscular imbalances, this can cause compensation injuries and long-term damage. These may either be front to back or side imbalances. For example, if a client's chest is more developed than his back, there may be a frontal curvature of the spine. This can lead to postural problems.

Flexibility is a fitness component that is allied with possible imbalances and injury. Here we define flexibility as the ability of a muscle to move through a range of motion. All clients should have a degree of flexibility training (stretching) within their programme. If the client exhibits a lack of flexibility, this may become a primary goal for the programme.

Also central is the concept of **intensity**. This is the level of training stress set for the client. Each client needs to be placed on a low-, medium- or high-intensity programme following careful analysis of what is appropriate for the individual. It is vital to make ongoing checks of the actual intensity level experienced by the client in order to ensure that it is neither too taxing (exhaustion) nor insufficiently taxing (in which case the alarm phase would be inadequately triggered).

Client needs analysis

A needs analysis should be completed at the initial consultation with a client and repeated at intervals during their training year. Examples of a need for a re-evaluation will be goal achievement, an injury or illness, or a change in the client's circumstances.

Needs analysis should ascertain the following information:

- Goals – primary, secondary and tertiary, both client and trainer based (Chapter 5 provides more detail on this topic).
- Training status – is the client currently training? If so, it is important to ascertain the type, length of recent participation, level of intensity and the resistance training status.
- Injuries/illness – details need to be recorded (for a discussion of record-keeping, see Chapter 6).
- Exercise history – this can be divided into time frames. For example, the following categories may be used: beginner (<2 months, low training stress, little training experience), transitional (2–6 months, medium training stress, some training knowledge), and advanced (>6 months, higher-intensity workouts, training knowledge).
- Protocols – does the client require the use of one or more protocol? A protocol is a recommended course of action for a programme, for example, if the client has high blood pressure, certain exercises are recommended.
- Fitness testing data (for details, see Chapter 8).
- Sport-specific training – does this need to be incorporated in the client's workout?

Once the needs analysis is complete, the PT can begin the exercise selection process. Inexperienced PTs can feel daunted by the sheer number of exercises available. When the range of exercises is combined with the range of equipment available, the task selection can become almost overwhelming. Chapter 7 helps here by showing a methodical approach: how to build exercise depth charts so that different exercises may be used to target the same muscle groups.

Exercise selection

The essential factors of exercise selection are location, the availability of equipment and the functional capacity of the client. These will vary significantly according to circumstances. Home training provides particular challenges for the PT, as does the degree of gym (in-house) training equipment. Time is a further factor in exercise selection: some clients may only have 30 minutes available for the whole session, though most sessions will last 45 minutes to 1 hour. The PT also needs to consider in advance what equipment will be available. It is helpful to consider how one piece of equipment may substitute for another, if the desired piece is unavailable for some reason.

Reflection 2.1

One of the often-overlooked factors of exercise selection are the client's preferences. If clients do not like a particular exercise or piece of equipment, they will not necessarily tell you – so you must ask. I have witnessed a trainer programme a treadmill session to every one of his clients just because he himself was a runner! PTs need to remember that it is the clients they are catering for, not themselves.

Exercise order

The general programming order of exercise should be:

warm-up ⇨ main body ⇨cool-down ⇨ flexibility.

A further component sometimes used is pre-stretch. Because some research indicates that a pre-stretch before resistance training may reduce muscular power output, this has been omitted (see Power et al., 2004 for a starting point). Within sessions it is entirely permissible to use a pre-main body stretch after the warm-up as the client may want a passive stretch as part of the service.

After the initial phase, cardiovascular training usually precedes resistance training if they are used in the same session. This is due to the additional warm-up aspect of CV training. Resistance training typically has the following exercise structure:

power ⇨ core (multi-joint) ⇨ isolating (single-joint).

Power exercises use momentum at phases of action, for example, power clean and push press (illustrated in Chapter 7 on pp102 and 103). In multi-joint exercises more than one joint is moving, e.g. squats (p89), chest press (pp92 and 93) and bent-over row (p94). Examples of single-joint exercises are bicep curl (p100), tricep extension (p101) and leg curl.

The PT can manipulate the sequence to some extent. For example, it is possible to move power exercises pre-CV as they need a high degree of muscular control. It is also possible to move isolating to pre-core exercises. Pre-fatigue sets would be an example: the PT pre-fatigues the client's pectorals with flyes before a chest press. Pre-fatigue is used when the PT wants to ensure that the larger muscles in a compound activity are fatigued (compound activity is where more than one muscle and joint are used to complete the movement). In the case of chest press it is sometimes necessary to pre-fatigue the pectorals as the triceps are smaller muscles and in some clients will fatigue more quickly. This will lead to the pectorals not being fatigued in those sets, unless they are pre-fatigued by means of an isolating exercise.

The components that should not be moved are (a) warm-up, (b) power and (c) cool-down as there are safety considerations here. A warm-up is essential to any programme and ideally should last at least five minutes. The intensity can be at the lower end of the target heart rate zone (heart rate measurement is explained below) – usually around 120 beats per minute (BPM). This will warm the soft tissues in preparation for the more intense work to come. It also allows the client to prepare psychologically for the tasks ahead. Any equipment mode may be used for the warm-up. An upper-body workout will require rowing or an upper body ergometer, whereas a sprint programme will require a treadmill or jogging.

The cool-down is as important for reducing the heart rate slowly to a safe value (typically below 120 BPM). This will normally be achievable in less than five minutes, though the length of time will depend on the intensity of the preceding workout. The client may need to cool down for longer, especially if they are hypertensive (i.e. have high blood pressure).

Frequency and volume

Frequency of training is dependent on the client's goals and programme structure. For example, for a client whose primary goal is improved health, a CV programme over consecutive days may be appropriate because they may be working at a moderate intensity. However, if a client is working on a 'general' resistance pro-gramme (working all muscle groups in a session), then that client will require a rest day in- between sessions and may work out three times per week. A bodybuilding client can be trained six days a week using a split routine (working different muscle groups on different days) and, with careful planning, be trained twice per day. The general guidelines are that there should be one rest day between sessions, but no more than three days if optimum gains are required.

The main factor for the PT will be the number of sessions with a PT that the client can afford to fit into a week. Clients may ask to be trained by the PT once a week with other sessions programmed for them to complete on their own. *Every* programme should have an expiry date provided by the PT. If the programme is adhered to, the adaptation in the client will usually cope with the intensity within approximately 4–6 weeks of the start of the programme. The client can then be given a fresh programme. Programmes with expiry dates have benefits to both parties: they are an aid to motivation for the client and help in client retention for the PT.

Avoiding overtraining

Overtraining occurs when the body enters the resistance phase (described in Selye's GAS model on pp7–8) and further training occurs before the physiological adaptation has been completed. Athletes and exercise-obsessive clients are the most at risk of overtraining. Athletes need careful programme planning as they are looking for optimum gains. This is where periodisation (an advanced form of programming) is used.

Periodised programmes break sessions down into very specific parts. This usually means that for every day of an athlete's career they know what they are doing in each training session. This is always the best method to employ when training athletes, although the periodised plans must be carefully constructed to reduce the likelihood of overtraining. More information on periodised programmes is given in Chapter 9.

Reflection 2.2

PTs need to be alert to indicators of overtraining. I have trained an obsessive exerciser and it became obvious that the client was actually going backwards with respect to training goals. This client was female, 39 years of age and extremely fit. (In fact, she was also a part-time aerobics instructor.) The sessions I took with her were always high intensity and if she ever missed a session she wanted to work twice as hard the next session. Her primary goal was to increase her aerobic fitness and to this end her overtraining markers were mood disturbances, decreased aerobic performance and increased muscle soreness. The immune system is suppressed during overtraining and this can lead to the client exhibiting an increased incidence of illness, as in fact she did. An interesting allied marker for this client was her nutritional intake. Invariably the total calorific intake was never enough to sustain her workouts. In this case I politely declined to train her further and advised her to take my counsellor referral recommendation.

Approaches

Cardiovascular training modes

CV training is used to overload the components of the cardio (heart) and vascular (arteries, capillaries and veins) system. The modes of CV training all achieve similar outcomes provided that the required intensity is reached. CV training is used to help lower body fat, increase aerobic fitness and increase the amount of oxygen the body can utilise. It is therefore ideal for improving specific aerobic fitness for athletes for competition and also for use in a general health programme. A wide variety of cardiovascular (CV) equipment is now available. Indoor cycles, rowers, cross-trainers, climbers, steppers and treadmills are just some of the modes that may be programmed. Programming should be as client-specific as possible. Programming detailed treadmill sessions to a cyclist, for example, may not be entirely appropriate.

The science behind CV training relates not so much to the mode of the activity as to the intensity, duration and rest periods within the programme. All CV programming is primarily concerned with energy system utilisation. There are three main types of CV programmes that may be used with your clients: continuous training, interval training and fartlek.

Continuous training

This involves using a warm-up followed by sustained intensity (steady state) for a period of time. This means that the client's heart rate may be increased to a level

Figure 2.2: Example of heart rate response to continuous training

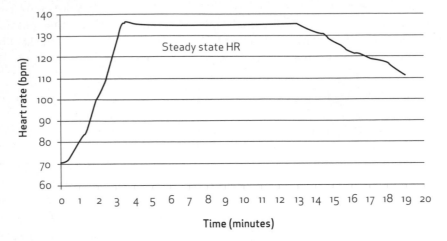

prescribed by the PT and kept at this level for the duration of the session. One problem that may occur with continuous training is boredom as the client pounds out a monotonous programme. This model may be most appropriate to new exercisers as it does not require changes in heart rate and higher intensities.

Interval training

The theory behind interval training is that, with the implementation of work and rest periods, the client can train for a higher intensity than in continuous training. This allows for greater energy expenditure over the workout time and a greater level of overload.

There are specific interval periods that correspond to the energy system being worked. The higher the intensity, the more rest is needed between repetitions. The various energy systems are explained in more detail in Chapter 3.

The following heart rate intensity guide figures (maximum heart rate – MHR) indicate a range of heart rates that clients may be trained at. Each should be tailored to the individual requirements and to the health status of the individual client.

Figure 2.3: Examples of heart rate response to interval training

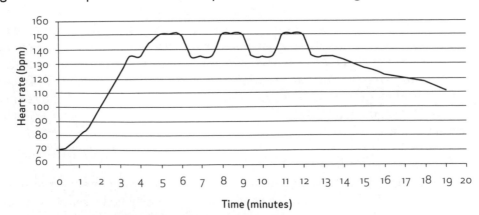

Figure 2.4: Energy system manipulation variables

Energy system	Work: rest	Work duration	Rest duration	Reps in session
ATP-PC	1:3	10 seconds	30 seconds	25
Anaerobic Glycolysis	1:2	30–120 seconds	60–240 seconds	15
Aerobic	1:1	120–300 seconds	120–300 seconds	5

This table is meant to be a guide only and can be manipulated accordingly within sessions.

- ATP-PC = >90 per cent.
- Anaerobic glycolysis = 80–90 per cent.
- Aerobic = 60–80 per cent.

Reflection 2.3

I trained two clients back-to-back of the same age and with similar health attributes. They were both male, 28 years old and asymptomatic (i.e. without symptoms – they did not exhibit any health problems). One could work at around 70 per cent MHR and the other could cope with 85 per cent MHR. The sessions were tailored to the functional capacity of each client.

Fartlek

'Fartlek' means speed play. This type of training should be purely random. There should be no structure to the timings of heart rate changes. Fartlek is especially applicable for team sports, most of which demonstrate high-intensity activity on an intermittent and irregular basis.

Figure 2.5: Example of heart rate response to fartlek training

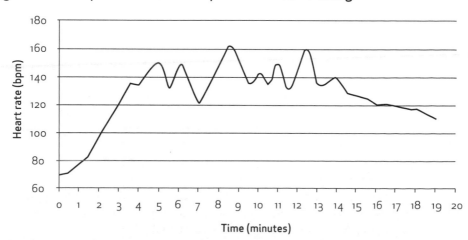

Activity 2.1

Plan three different CV training sessions with warm-up and cool-down using the following guidelines:

1. Fartlek training on a treadmill, 25 minutes in duration, for a footballer.
2. Continuous training on a stepper for 15 minutes for a sedentary client.
3. Interval training on a rower for 20 minutes to work the aerobic energy system.

Methods of resistance training

There are many different methods of resistance training. The main methods are as follows:

- **Straight sets**: (a) single set – one set is performed in each exercise, which is entirely appropriate for beginners; (b) multiple sets, e.g. three sets – it is widely recognised that multiple sets elicit greater adaptation in muscle tissue.
- **Pyramid sets**: either ascending or descending. For example, three sets performed in ascending order of intensity (or load) – 10 reps at 70 kg, 8 reps at 80 kg and 6 reps at 90 kg.
- **Super sets**: there are two versions of this method. The PT can (a) get their client to perform bicep curls immediately followed by tricep extensions, thereby 'super setting' the agonist (prime contracting muscle in the exercise) and antagonist (secondary counteracting muscle); or (b) use multiple successive exercises for the same muscle group, such as chest press followed by chest flyes followed by press-ups. This will lead to complete fatigue in that muscle group.
- **Negatives**: this programme uses eccentric muscle contraction to overload muscle tissue beyond what the client can normally lift. It is therefore a high-intensity tool for use if the client is capable of coping. The PT helps the client with the initial lift and then allows them to 'control' the weight on the downward phase. For example, if a client is incapable of performing body weight chin-ups, the trainer can lift him or her up to the completed position for a chin-up and then get them to lower themselves slowly back down unassisted.
- **Drop sets**: with this method the load lifted in a single set is progressively lightened. It is easier using machines. For example, the client will perform 3 reps at 30 kg, 3 reps at 25 kg and 3 reps at 20 kg in the same set. It is also possible to lighten the load in subsequent sets if the client is unable to complete the initial weight. In this example the client may start the second set at 3 reps at 25 kg and move down to 3 reps at 20 kg and 3 reps at 15 kg.
- **Forced reps**: this is a high-intensity method and should be used only if the client is deemed capable. Once the client has completed the initial set to fatigue, the PT 'helps' them to perform further reps that are beyond their capability to perform by themselves (e.g. a bicep preacher curl is performed to fatigue and the PT then helps lift the dumb-bell for further reps).

- **Circuit type**: this involves the client performing different exercises in succession with timings from 30 seconds to 1 minute for each exercise performed and the same timed rest period between exercises. It is also possible to use repetitions as designated sets, for example, 15 reps then move on to the next exercise. The clients move around a circuit of exercises, repeating each exercise a number of times depending on the length of the session. Most PTs regard this method as a class type of activity, but it can be utilised in a gym environment just as well. It is particularly applicable when working for muscular endurance.
- **Split routine**: the client will work different muscle groups on different days, such as chest and back on Mondays, legs and shoulders on Tuesdays and arms and abs (abdominals)/lower back on Wednesdays, then repeat the cycle over the next three days. This allows the muscle groups to be worked harder in each available session and allows the client to work out on consecutive days relatively safely.

Free weights and machines

The decision over whether to use free weights or resistance machines will depend on the type of client and the availability of equipment. Generally, free weights make a higher neuromuscular demand as a result of the 'control' element to the movement. Some exercises can be performed only by using free weights, for example, a barbell power clean (illustrated on pp102–3). A client can also perform multi-plane action (see below) and everyday activities with free weights. Free weights are not constrained by having a set movement pattern: you can move in many directions in the same exercise (for example, a kettlebell one-arm row into shoulder press would be impossible using resistance machines). Free weights are generally much more flexible to use than machines.

Resistance machines do offer a safety feature if failure occurs: they will 'catch' the weight for the client. The use of cams (curved pulleys to maximise work that are found on most machines) will also benefit resistance through most if not all of the range of movement (ROM) on a machine. A machine can also offer inexperienced clients a less intimidating prospect in early sessions, at least until they gain confidence to take your advice and move on to free weight exercises. Cable machines offer aspects of both resistance machines and free weights. They offer safety and different planes of movement in one machine, as well as a multitude of exercises with different attachments.

Planes of movement

The three planes of movement are:

- sagittal (a vertical plane passing from front to rear, cutting the body into two symmetrical halves, i.e. in line with the nose);
- frontal (at right angles to the sagittal plane, this cuts the body from the side in line with the arms);
- transverse (horizontal plane cutting the body across the middle).

Single plane relates to movement in only one of these planes, for example, a lat pulldown is in the frontal plane. Multi-plane refers to movement in two or more planes, for example, a baseball bat swing is in all three planes.

Functional training

The term 'functional training' (FT) is widely used in the fitness industry. Functional training uses exercises to reproduce, and thereby improve, everyday movements. For example, the woodchop cable exercise mimics the chopping of a tree. (The term 'functional' thus relates both to the ability to perform everyday tasks and to an exercise outcome which performs a specific 'function'.) One clear use of functional training is in a rehabilitation context.

Some trainers extol the virtues of FT to the extent of disregarding many other training methods. However, problems can occur when trainers use exercise techniques and a variety of equipment that train clients in what they deem to be a functional manner. This can include the use of 'bosu' balls, gymnastic balls, foam rollers, wobble boards and all manner of unstable equipment. The idea is that the PT uses multi-plane and unstable exercises to work the 'core' musculature of the client or the session can be manipulated by the PT to provide exercises more applicable to normal life. Indeed, there is a heightened stimulation of the neuromuscular junctions in the muscles used during FT, but is this really necessary? If a client's primary goal is to build muscle for aesthetic reasons, does FT need to be used at all? The answer should be to use FT only to work on muscle balance, rehabilitation activities, to provide variety in some sessions or to target a client's low functional capacity to perform everyday tasks. Always work from the client needs analysis, and think carefully before employing one approach to the exclusion of others.

Reflection 2.4

I have seen entire sessions where a trainer has used an unstable surface for the client to train on. The question I have thought at the time is why? How many clients actually walk or play on an unstable surface in everyday tasks? And how many require the use of unstable surfaces in their sport? Not many! Functional exercises should be used only when it will provide adaptation to the client's primary, secondary or tertiary goals. A good example would be a softball player using a cable machine to provide resistance when 'picking up a ground ball' in a gym environment.

Note too that there are safety considerations when using unstable surfaces. Gymnastic balls are an example. They have been known to burst under pressure. If this happens when your client is performing chest press with a 20 kg dumb-bell in each hand, the result will be quite nasty. The ability to lift repetition maximums will also be compromised if chest press is performed on a ball, so the question is: why do it at all?

Using programming tools

Intensity guidelines

Experience suggests that many PTs do not measure exercise intensity when training their clients. How, then, can they possibly know what intensity the client is at? Does the trainer merely rely on how the client looks? Or does the trainer guess? As explained in the chapter on session planning (Chapter 6), you should check at various intervals during the session. There are three main methods for measuring intensity:

- **heart rate monitors**: these are now inexpensive and can be linked to a personal computer to track intensity in sessions;
- **heart rate palpation**: this involves manually taking the pulse at intervals in the workout. Use a ten-second count and multiply by six to obtain a beats per minute (BPM) reading.
- **rating of perceived exertion (RPE):** here the client is asked to describe subjectively how intense they feel an activity to be. There is a choice of scales for rating client response. (The scale I prefer is the 6–20 numbered scale, as it can be related to the client's heart rate when a zero is added to the figure given.)

Reflection 2.5

I tailor the intensity measurement to the client and/or the session. Heart rate monitors are useful for tracking higher-intensity athlete clients. Palpation can be more appropriate for use with the general population. On rare occasions I have felt a potentially dangerous arrhythmia and have referred the client to their GP. RPE is used as a supplement to palpation and is surprisingly accurate with experienced clients. It is especially relevant when used with hypertensive clients who are on medication, as their heart rates are artificially lowered. RPE is also useful when gauging the difficulty experienced by clients when resistance training. Remember that they should be fatiguing on every set performed and should be giving you a high RPE number when checked. There may be a difference between perception and reality when using RPE charts. There are clients who will give an estimate of 18 when the heart rate indicates 13. Usually this means that they do not want to work very hard. Conversely, I have known the 'male ego' client who places himself at 10 on the scale when he really means 16! You need to try to ensure that the client is being truthful when using RPE. If you suspect a client of under- or over-estimating an RPE figure, consider the useful insight this may provide into their individual thinking and motivation.

The PT should work out the client's intensity heart rate zones during the initial consultation. These heart rate zones (HRZ) will be determined by the current status of the client. A low, moderate or high HRZ can be assigned depending on their functional capacity. The easiest and quickest method is to use the estimate of the client's maximum heart rate (220 minus age) and then

Reflection 2.5 continued

work out a percentage of that figure. For example, if a client was capable of moderate intensity work, then you will calculate 70 per cent of their estimated maximum heart rate and this will be the ceiling heart rate that you will use in your programme.

A more client-specific approach is to use the Karvonen method. You will need to understand resting heart rate for this method. Resting heart rate is exactly that: the beats per minute of the heart at rest. The only issue is the definition of rest. For your purposes, the easiest method is to get your client to sit quietly for five minutes, then take a full minute reading of their pulse. You can then use this figure in the Karvonen method of estimating THRZ (target heart rate zone). Work out the client's maximum heart rate (MHR) as above; then subtract their resting heart rate (RHR); then work out their percentage target heart rate zone (THRZ); and then add the RHR onto those figures. The definitions of THRZ that you can use vary slightly between PTs. I use low, moderate and high heart rate (HR) intensity brackets as follows:

- low: 50–65 per cent;
- moderate: 65–75 per cent;
- high: >75 per cent.

Here is a worked example. Client 1 is male and 22 years of age with an RHR of 60 BPM. He has an estimated MHR of 198 BPM (220 – 22 years). If his THRZ was 65–85 per cent of MHR, then, using the first method, the calculations would be:

$$198 \times 0.65 = 129 \text{ BPM}$$
$$198 \times 0.85 = 168 \text{ BPM}$$

His THRZ, therefore, would equal 129–168 BPM in his sessions. Applying the Karvonen method, you record his RHR as 60 BPM. This would produce the following calculation:

$$198 \text{ BPM} – 60 \text{ BPM} = 138 \text{ BPM} \times 0.65$$
$$198 \text{ BPM} – 60 \text{ BPM} = 138 \text{ BPM} \times 0.85$$

This would result in 90 and 117 BPM. Adding 60 RHR produces a final THRZ of 150 – 177 BPM. As you can see, this is higher than the previous 'quick' method because the client has a relatively low resting heart rate.

Activity 2.2

Use both of the above methods to calculate the THRZ for the following clients:

1. Female, 46 years of age and an RHR of 75 BPM (moderate intensity, 70 per cent).
2. Male, 19 years of age and an RHR of 57 BPM (high intensity, 85 per cent).
3. Female, 26 years of age and an RHR of 63 BPM (moderate intensity, 65 per cent).

Repetition ranges

Knowledge of repetition ranges is vital. This enables the PT to determine the desired outcome of training programmes. Fibre type recruitment and energy system utilisation are both affected by rep ranges. Muscle fibre types are recruited (utilised by muscle) by manipulating rep ranges. There are three main types of muscle fibres: type I (aerobic), type IIa (intermediate) and type IIb (anaerobic). Different fibre types can be recruited using different rep ranges, for example, higher muscular endurance reps will recruit more aerobic type fibres, whereas lower power reps will recruit more anaerobic type fibres. One way to understand the effect of rep ranges is to view the number of reps programmed on a continuum:

Reps	1	3	5	7	9	11	13	15	17	19*

| **Effect** | Power | Strength | | Hypertrophy | Endurance |

* Even rep numbers are omitted for illustrative purposes only

Note that when using this continuum, each training effect will affect other rep ranges. For example, if your client trains for hypertrophy, then there will be some effect on strength and endurance capabilities and, to a lesser extent, power. We distinguish these terms as follows:

- Power = work/time. This is related to muscle size and the ability to generate muscular velocity.
- Strength = the maximum amount that your client can lift in one repetition.
- Hypertrophy = increasing muscle fibre size and therefore muscle size.
- Endurance = the ability to sustain repetitions.

Rep ranges are related to the load lifted. Obviously, the heavier the weight, the fewer reps your client can perform. *All* rep ranges should be viewed as repetition maximums (RMs). For example, a client who can perform 10 barbell chest presses at 40 kg should not be able to perform a full eleventh rep. Fatigue should occur on every set.

Figure 2.6: Relationship between training variables and effects

Energy systems exercise duration effects

Predominant energy systems		
ATP ATP-PC	Anaerobic glycolysis	Aerobic

Time →

| 0 secs   10 secs | 1 minute | 2 minutes | 3 minutes |

Javelin 100m Sprint	400m	800m	1500m
Discus	200m swim		400m swim
Weightlifting			
Sporting examples			

Muscle fibre type recruitment		
Type IIB	Type IIA	Type I
White	Pink	Red
Glycolytic	Oxidative/glycolytic	Oxidative

Repetitions →

1 2 3 4 5 6 7 8 9 10 11 12 13 14 15 16 17 18 19 20

Power	Strength	Hypertrophy	Endurance
Primary muscle adaption			

As Figure 2.6 shows, rep ranges are also interrelated with muscle fibre types, sports and energy systems. This figure is useful as a quick reference guide when programming rep ranges for your clients. If you were to programme reps incorrectly, you could make it harder for your client to reach his or her primary goal.

Another method of programming up or down from your client's known rep ranges is to use 1 RM tables. RM (repetition maximum) is the maximum amount of reps that a client can perform with a particular weight before they fatigue. As long as you know a particular RM (for example, a 1 RM weight performed by your client), you can then look up what the client *should* be performing at 10 RM. An example would be a client who can lift 100 kg for 1 RM on a barbell squat: according to this method, they could perform 75 kg for 10 RM.

Activity 2.3

A new male client comes to you and, through your client analysis, you assign hypertrophy and aesthetic gain as the primary goals. Check Figure 2.6 and decide where you are going to focus his training.

Now do the same for a second new client, who is female and an 800 m runner for a local athletics club. Is she placed differently on Figure 2.6?

There are limitations to these tables, however: there is inter-client variability; the tables assume that only one set is being performed; and they do not differentiate between resistance machines and the use of comparable free weights. There is a web address at the end of this chapter that will provide 1 RM tables. Try visiting the site and using the tables to answer the following:

- What is the 10 RM if your client can lift 61 kg for 5 reps?
- What is the 3 RM if your client can lift 46 kg for 15 reps?

Sets

The number of sets to be programmed also needs to be scientifically based. The basic guidelines are:

- power = 3–5 sets;
- strength = 2–6 sets;
- hypertrophy = 3–6 sets;
- endurance = 2–3 sets.

As you can see, these guidelines provide a range of sets for use in programming. They act only as guides: different programme goals will require different set numbers. For example, a client on a split routine may utilise a higher set number as the time spent on an exercise will be greater. Another factor that may affect the set number is client response. Each client responds differently to differing stimuli. As you train your client you can constantly update the programme accordingly.

Rest periods between sets

These are determined by the training rep range and effect as follows:

- power requires 2–5 minutes;
- strength requires 2–5 minutes;
- hypertrophy requires 30–90 seconds;
- endurance requires <30 seconds.

Reflection 2.6

One fitness trainer approached me and asked, 'How do I programme rest periods between sets?' This took me aback at first as I assumed that this was essential knowledge that any trainer would know. I later discovered that the problem here was the advent of electronic resistance machines programming the rest periods! While it is fine to use innovative equipment, you need to know the fundamentals first.

Muscle balance

This is an often neglected aspect of exercise programming. Many clients will train 'what they can see'. For example, men are fond of chest and bicep brachii training, while often neglecting the back and triceps. To reduce agonist (prime contracting muscle in an exercise) and antagonist (secondary counteracting muscle) strength imbalances, use the following muscle balance ratios:

- Chest : back = 2:3
- Quadriceps : hamstrings = 3:2
- Abdominals : lower back = 1:1
- Bicep : tricep = 1:1
- Gastrocnemius : tibialis anterior = 3:1

For example, to promote a strength ratio of chest:back of 2:3, a client performs two sets of ten reps for chest and three sets of ten for the back. These ratios are a guide; some research supports slightly different ratios (see **www.brianmac.co.uk/ sambc.htm**). The key point is that all body parts should be trained on both sides of the body to promote a balanced muscular system.

Reflection 2.7

One client I worked with was male and very muscular. He looked like a bodybuilder and trained at a high intensity. It became obvious, however, that his 'core' muscles were inadequate to support his level of aesthetic weight training. One day he injured his back and then spent many weeks rehabilitating and strengthening his core. Personal trainers should promote muscle balancing wherever possible. This can be difficult when a client wants only to train the chest or thighs. In such a case you must do your ethical duty and advise the client to train the other body parts in sessions with you or, at the very least, in their unsupervised sessions.

Flexibility

If the client exhibits lack of flexibility, then stretching will take up a large proportion of the session. Training for development or maintenance of flexibility involves the range of motion (ROM) of a joint. Flexibility should be programmed alongside other methods of training. Research into stretching is inconclusive as to whether it actually reduces the incidence of injury. It is prudent to work from a perspective that decreased ROM will increase the risk of injury, especially in sporting activity.

Stretching training uses duration and sets in the same way as other training aspects. Some research indicates that the length of time of hold of the stretch has a bearing on the adaptation. The ACSM (2007) recommends that each stretch should be held for 30–90 seconds. Some evidence suggests that the stretch should be held for 10 seconds for maintenance of ROM. You must use your judgement when programming stretching, as using 90 seconds for every muscle group in your client would take up a large proportion of their whole session.

The stretch reflex

This relates to two physiological properties of muscle tissue, namely, muscle spindles and golgi tendon organs (GTOs). Muscle spindles are within the muscle fibres and are concerned with muscle length. If the muscle spindle 'fires' a reflex action, the muscle has been taken past its normal operating length and the reflex is to contract. This is called the stretch reflex. The GTO measures muscle tension and, unsurprisingly, is located in the tendon of each muscle. If tension becomes too great, the GTO 'fires' and the muscle will relax, therefore reducing tension. This is termed 'muscular inhibition'.

Flexibility can be active (the ROM available under muscular contraction, that is, how far the client can take a stretch) or passive (the ROM available when an external force pushes the client into a particular stretch).

Different methods of stretching are:

- **Static** (active): the client adopts the stretch position and holds the stretch themselves for the predetermined length of time. These are most appropriate when stretching alone.
- **Dynamic** (active): this method usually involves movements that mimic sport movements that are due to be made in a sporting context. It can also be useful in warm-ups generally.
- **Ballistic** (active): bouncing of the joint and musculature within a stretch. These are recommended only for more advanced athlete-type clients as they provide ROM beyond normal ranges.
- **Passive**: a PT puts the client into the stretch and provides the necessary force to elicit the stretch in the muscle. Communication between the client and the PT is paramount, as you only want to take the stretch to a safe limit. The client should inform you when they can feel a strong stretch – no more. Passive stretching is particularly appropriate in PT sessions as the client is paying for a service and this method of stretching should be part of it.
- **Proprioceptive neuromuscular facilitation** (PNF) (passive/active): this method usually requires the help of the trainer and is applicable when maximum adaptation of the client's flexibility is required. An example is a lying hamstring stretch performed by the trainer (passive in the client), then the client pushes against the trainer with the hamstrings (active in the client), then the trainer stretches the client further. It utilises the stretch reflex to allow the GTO to fire during the active phase which allows the muscle to relax further in the passive phase, therefore producing a greater ROM. There are other PNF methods: it is recommended that you read around this method of stretching. A good place to start for examples is McAtee's *Facilitated stretching* (2007).

Activity 2.4

1. Start by practising actively stretching your quadriceps, hamstrings, triceps, calves, chest and back.
2. Next move on to dynamic stretching by choosing a sport and mimicking the main actions. For instance, in football the kicking of an imaginary ball would be applicable.

Activity 2.4 continued

3. Only practise ballistic stretching if you are capable.
4. When you are confident with the concept of stretching, try passive stretching on a willing participant. Tread carefully and only take the stretch to a safe point. See **www.personaltraining1st.com** for some examples of passive stretching.
5. Research PNF stretching and when you have some experience of passive stretching in a professional environment, practise this technique so that you can utilise it when necessary.

Active learning

The practical element of this chapter is paramount when applying your programming knowledge. If you are starting out as a PT you need to gain experience through writing programmes. One method is to invent clients to programme for. When you attempt this, try to start with straightforward programmes and progress to more advanced clients. This will boost your confidence when tackling real life programming. Think about the many options when you write these programmes – you can use Chapter 7 in this book to help you choose exercises and move on to advanced training techniques information (Chapter 9) when you feel ready.

Reflection 2.8

When I was starting out, other trainers were themselves a great resource. I took part in many group discussions about new exercises and effective training methods for a variety of clients. Use the fitness professionals you know as sounding boards for your ideas and soak up their thoughts in order to critique your own practice.

Summary

With the information provided in this chapter, you should now have a good grasp of the importance of basing all fitness programming on sound scientific research. Remember, the purpose of this chapter is to give you an introductory guide to the writing and implementation of professional programmes. There are two main considerations that you will need always to bear in mind. First, research within exercise and fitness is constantly being updated and programming is one of the fastest changing subjects in this area. Personal trainers need to continue reading research to ensure that their programming skills are up to date. Journals such as the ACSM's *Health and Fitness* and *Peak Performance* (available online at **www.pp-online.co.uk**) will provide up-to-date fitness information. The other aspect is that scientific understanding needs actually to be applied in practice at every opportunity. PTs are only as good as their last programmes!

Above all, programmes need to be 'SPARS':

1. Safe.
2. Prepared using science.
3. Achievable.
4. Recorded.
5. Specific.

Further study

Explore the key NSCA texts: *Essentials of strength training and conditioning* (Baechle and Earle, 2000) and *Essentials of personal training* (Baechle and Earle, 2003). *ACSM's resources for the personal trainer* (ACSM, 2004) gives in-depth information on programming for health in the general population.

For more on resistance training, see *Designing resistance training programmes* (Fleck and Kraemer, 2003).

For general PT programming information visit: **www.personaltraining1st.com**

For RPE charts see the ACSM on RPE charts and usage: **www.acsm.org/Content/ContentFolders/Publications/CurrentComment/2001/perceive103101.pdf**

Polar HR online software – Polar provides a free online service to upload heart rate monitoring data. Registration is required to access this service: **www.polarpersonal trainer.com/frontend/**

1 RM tables – **www.depauw.edu/ath/strength/Images/Estimating%201RM%20and %20Training%20Loads.pdf**

Stretching guidelines – **www.pponline.co.uk/encyc/stretching-performance-and-injury-prevention**

For a general summary of stretching research see **www.exrx.net/Lists/Directory. html**. This link provides stretches for most muscles; just click on the area to be stretched.

Periodisation – **www.brianmac.co.uk/plan.htm** has a general guide to periodisation with other links to specific sports.

www.tennis.se/files/%7B6C0150F2-D618-4568-8F05-D958E682462B%7D.pdf is an excellent document from the international tennis federation regarding extensive periodising for tennis players.

Chapter 3

Adaptations to physiology

How does physiology apply to training clients? Why should a prospective or current PT be interested in physiology? The answer is simple: as everything a PT does should be based on a scientific approach, physiology is central to everyday training life. In the past, sports coaches and trainers could come from a sports background with little or no scientific knowledge. This is no longer the case. Consider the coaches and trainers you know: how many are still unqualified? PTs today need to understand the link between training programmes and clients' physiological adaptation.

This chapter provides a concise and accessible introduction to the subject. Obviously, no single chapter on this subject can be comprehensive. However, a wealth of resources is available and a number of these are listed at the end of the chapter for further study. It is important for PTs to focus their study on the *application* of information to their training of various clients. It is helpful to keep considering how what you learn about physiology may be applied to the training of the two main client categories, namely, health clients and athletes.

For the purposes of teaching, physiology is often divided into separate systems. In practice, however, it is important to think holistically – to consider how these different systems work together during training.

This chapter is designed to help you:

- recognise the direct link between programming and physiology;
- understand that all physiological systems may be affected by training;
- become familiar with the relevant physiological systems;
- appreciate that each client will react differently to training stimulus.

Physiology is a branch of science that is concerned with the functions of the human body. Often physiology is discussed in a medical context. For the purpose of explaining the adaptation of physiology to training, the following systems will be discussed:

- Energy.
- Neuromuscular.
- Cardiovascular.
- Respiratory.

- Endocrine (hormones).
- Skeletal.

Energy systems

Energy systems influence every aspect of a client's overall fitness. Every training session will involve the manipulation of energy systems using duration and intensity to bring about changes and to build these into chronic (long-lasting) adaptations. Energy supply in the human body can be viewed on a time continuum. This is shown in Figure 3.1.

Here the first type of energy is provided by adenosine triphosphate (ATP). This source of energy is used up rapidly (within around two seconds) during exercise. The second source of energy is the ATP-PC (phosphagen) system. This provides energy for up to about 8–10 seconds. Then anaerobic glycolysis will provide energy during the next stage, from approximately 10 seconds to one minute (anaerobic energy being that which does not require a release of oxygen). Increasingly, this is supported by energy from aerobic glycolysis, which will supply energy for up to about three minutes (aerobic energy being that which requires release of oxygen). Finally, aerobic systems (i.e. those requiring oxygen) become the predominant provider of energy. A note is needed on fuel for these energy systems. Anaerobic glycolysis requires carbohydrate and aerobic energy systems require fat (lipids) with a small amount of protein being used when needed.

The main point to remember here is that no one energy system is working alone. (If your aerobic system did not 'tick over' you would be working totally anaerobically and would, in fact, be dead!) The body utilises oxygen to maintain its metabolism (metabolism being the chemical processes occurring within the body). Figure 3.1 shows how at various points during a period of continuous activity various energy systems work in tandem. PTs are interested in the points where energy systems cross over. The two main points are 10 seconds (with anaerobic glycolysis becoming predominant) and around one minute (with aerobic systems becoming predominant).

Figure 3.1: Energy system usage relative to time in physical ctivity

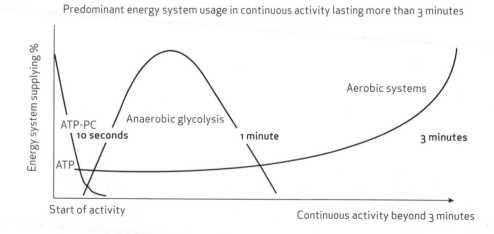

Predominant energy system usage in continuous activity lasting more than 3 minutes

Energy system supplying %

ATP-PC
10 seconds
Anaerobic glycolysis
1 minute
Aerobic systems
3 minutes
ATP

Start of activity

Continuous activity beyond 3 minutes

Figure 3.1 provides the basis of the PT's knowledge for anaerobic and aerobic energy system training. It is helpful to relate this to the continuum illustrated in Figure 2.2 on p14, which shows the impact of various sporting activities. Note that differences in training the two groups of clients (health clients and athletes) are relative to duration and intensity, rather than absolute differences. Workout session record sheets (see pp75–6) can be used to monitor the energy systems being trained.

Activity 3.1

First, here are some worked examples.

Q. Lisa is a health client. Her goal is to improve her overall 'fitness'. There is no need to programme high intensity for this client. Which predominant energy system training would you target for her?

A. Training should target the aerobic energy system as she has no need for power or sport-specific adaptations. A PT could work her up to around 70–85 per cent of her maximum heart rate and stay within the necessary aerobic zone. This will increase her overall aerobic fitness as well as having other health benefits.

Q. Naomi is an amateur 400 m runner. Based on previous test data, her goal is to increase her anaerobic threshold. She will require different intensity guidelines from Lisa. What energy systems would you programme for Naomi?

A. Anaerobic glycolysis should be the preferred system here. The lactate threshold is the point at which blood lactate starts to increase above baseline levels (known as OBLA – onset of blood lactate) and is particularly noticeable in events like the 400 m race. OBLA marks the onset of symptoms such as nausea and muscle fatigue, and will lead to a rapid decrease in performance. A PT will want to keep Naomi working around that anaerobic threshold (80–90 per cent of maximum heart rate). This will produce high amounts of lactic acid and her body will adapt to cope with higher levels of lactic acid with chronic training.

Now decide how to train the next two clients.

1. Jerome is a 100 m sprinter. He needs to overload his energy systems in order to produce adaptation and decrease his overall 100 m time. Use Figure 3.1 to decide how to train him.
2. Ebony is a striker in an amateur football team. She wants to increase her speed and overall endurance during a match. Which energy systems need attention through training? (Remember that most team sports are characterised by intermittently high-intensity activity.)

There comes a point when 'graded' training necessitates a move out of aerobic energy system supply and back into the anaerobic systems. This is inevitable in all human beings. We cannot maintain high-intensity activity indefinitely. How long a client can produce energy to sustain muscular contraction via aerobic energy systems will depend on the individual's level of energy system fitness. A good example of the 'tipping' over into anaerobic systems occurs in the sprint finish shown by athletes in long-distance running. They have adapted their bodies to start using aerobic energy systems much more quickly than an average client. This means that they can 'save' some anaerobic energy until the final part of the race. This anaerobic 'threshold' is linked to a percentage of MHR and differs in each client according to energy system fitness.

Training adaptations

Chapter 2 provided a series of training recommendations regarding mode, intensity, duration and frequency in training programming. Here they may be linked to energy systems adaptations.

Training for the ATP and ATP-PC systems will:

- increase ATP stores;
- increase creatine stores (creatine is produced by the body and stored for use as energy in the phosphocreatine (PC) system);
- increase the activity of the creatine kinase and adenosine triphosphatase (ATPase) enzymes (these enzymes break chemical bonds which produce energy).

These adaptations will increase overall power capacity of the ATP-PC system.

Training for the anaerobic glycolysis system will:

- increase the storage of glucose (glycogen);
- increase the activity of anaerobic system enzymes phosphofructokinase (PFK) and glycogen phosphorolase (GPP) (these enzymes are involved in the utilisation of glucose for energy);
- increase the ability to deal with hydrogen ions via the increased usage of buffering systems (buffering systems will remove the hydrogen ions from the system and reduce the acidity of blood; examples of physiological buffers are bicarbonate and phosphate);
- increase glycolytic capacity (the benefit here is that the client will be able to break down glucose more efficiently);
- increase the time to the anaerobic threshold and the onset of blood lactate to allow longer duration activity at a higher intensity; decrease in the nausea and dizziness associated with OBLA above.

Training for the aerobic energy systems will:

- increase mitochondria in muscle cells (mitochondria are the 'powerhouses' of cells where aerobic metabolism occurs);
- increase in myoglobin which stores oxygen within the muscle;
- increase the use of lipids during activity;
- increase the storage and usage of aerobic system enzymes (e.g. lipoprotein lipase which helps to break down fat (triglycerides));
- make delivery of oxygen from haemoglobin to muscle tissues more efficient;
- decrease percentage body fat;
- increase capillary density within muscle tissue (capillaries are the smallest part of the vascular system and have walls only one cell thick in order to facilitate oxygen diffusion; by increasing the density of capillaries in muscle tissue, more oxygen will be available for utilisation);
- maximise the aerobic capacity of muscle fibres.

Training for the neuromuscular system

The neuromuscular system involves the interaction between the nervous and muscular systems. Understanding this relationship is necessary for a PT as human movement stems from the way the nervous system controls skeletal muscle. Adaptations will depend on the number of repetitions performed. Remember the repetition continuum figure in Chapter 2? The adaptation will occur in the muscle fibre that is being overloaded. The neuromuscular system, therefore, should be considered in endurance and anaerobic terms.

Muscular adaptations using endurance repetitions (>15 reps)

This type of training uses type IIa and type I fibres and targets aerobic, oxygen-reliant, systems. There will be little hypertrophy evident (i.e. the increase in muscle mass due to an increase in the size of muscle fibres). Imagine a client who works out using only circuit-based sessions. There will be morphological changes, but bodybuilding will not be one of them. Current thinking in exercise physiology is that there may be some changes in type IIb fibres to a more aerobic structure. There will also be an increase in capillary density within muscle tissue to supply the increased need for oxygenated blood. Oxygenated blood (oxygen-rich blood) is needed for the more aerobic muscle fibres to contract, since they use aerobic energy systems. If there is a lack of oxygenated blood, performance will be compromised. These changes will increase aerobic endurance at a moderate intensity.

Muscular adaptations using hypertrophy, strength and power repetitions (<15 reps)

Along with some morphological changes to type IIa fibres into more anaerobic fibre types, there will be an increase in:

- muscular strength;
- force production, therefore increasing total power output;
- total anaerobic power;
- muscle fibre size (hypertrophy);
- connective tissue strength (tendons and ligaments);
- lean body mass, including muscle mass (lean body mass is a person's total mass minus the fat);
- basal metabolic rate (basal metabolic rate (BMR) can be measured in kcal and is the minimum amount of kcal that a client will expend to maintain their current mass without moving; the more muscle mass a client has, the higher the BMR due to muscle tissue being metabolically active);
- bone mineral density.

Neurological (nervous system) changes related to the muscle adaptations

The nervous and muscular systems are interlinked. Consider weightlifting competitions: 'muscle memory' is evident as technique plays an important part of the lift. Success does not just depend on the strength of the athlete. The athlete's motor units within activated muscles during the lift recall the movement pattern in the same way that clients' muscular systems do when they perform resistance training. After prolonged training the central nervous system will increase activation when training and there will be an improvement of the firing of motor units across the neuro-muscular junction (the point at which the nervous and muscular systems meet). This leads to an improved co-ordination between the central nervous system and motor units (essentially between the brain, nerves and the muscle tissue). The client's muscles will 'remember' the lifting pattern. This is why clients that are new to resistance training can improve the weight lifted very quickly: their muscles learn the lifting pattern before there are many strength changes.

Genetic predisposition

The adaptations that occur in the neuromuscular system are dependent on the fibre type that is predominant in your client. Every client will exhibit fibre types based on genetic make-up. This is termed their 'genetic predisposition' and cannot be changed. Adaptation can also be affected by the client's somatotype (body shape). There are three main types of somatotype. Endomorphs are short and stocky; mesomorphs are powerful and muscular; and ectomorphs are tall and thin.

Athletes tend to have a certain predominance of particular fibre types. Consider again Jerome, our 100 m sprinter: what type of fibres would he have an abundance of? He would have a higher proportion of type IIb anaerobic fibres, as these are recruited during a 100 m sprint. Compare this to Naomi, who wants to increase her anaerobic threshold during endurance events. She would probably be less muscular than Jerome: 400 m running recruits predominately type IIa fibres, similar glycolytic fibre types and a higher proportion of type I fibres.

While it is amazing what physical training can achieve, the outcomes are limited by a client's 'genetic potential'. This genetic ceiling will determine the maximum gains possible with each individual client. Even with elite athlete training, however, that genetic potential is rarely reached, so there is usually plenty of room for improvement for all clients!

Reflection 3.1

Having trained many different-shaped clients, I find the changes that can occur if they adhere to training and nutritional guidelines can be amazing. Problems can occur, however, when a client (usually in the minority) chooses to ignore almost all of the PT's recommendations and yet still expects to see significant changes. If you do come across one of these clients, the best course of action may be to try a period of training and, if the client does not progress in any way, then politely drop that client from your client base. This is an ethical course to take.

A note on flexibility

Flexibility training will elicit changes in connective and muscular tissues. Ligaments and tendons will allow a limited increase in range of movement (ROM) due to morphological changes in the soft tissues. The muscle fibres themselves will increase in residual length. This will also increase ROM within the muscle being stretched.

The stretch reflex involving muscle spindles will be inhibited to a greater degree. These muscle spindles are located within the muscle tissue itself and monitor muscle length. If the muscle over-lengthens, the muscle spindle will 'fire' and a stretch reflex will occur, thereby contracting the muscle. If this action is inhibited, the muscle can stretch further. Overall, these changes will increase the flexibility of the client, especially if you target the muscles that are in need of improvement.

Training for the cardiovascular (CV) system

While low-repetition resistance training does also produce some physiological changes to the CV system, this section will focus on endurance CV training adaptations. Endurance activities include rowing, running or swimming. The following changes occur within the heart or vascular systems and greatly enhance the efficiency of the cardiovascular system overall:

- increase in left ventricle hypertrophy (located within the heart);
- decrease in resting heart rate;
- increase in cardiac output (increased stroke volume);
- increase in ejection fraction of the heart (the ejection fraction representing the amount of blood that is pumped out of the left ventricle with each beat of the heart);
- improved oxygen capacity through increase in red blood cells and increased plasma volume;

- decrease in exercise heart rate at submaximal intensities;
- reduction in resting and exercising blood pressure;
- increased oxygen utilisation at muscle tissue sites;
- decrease in coronary disease risk factors;
- decrease in body fat percentage;
- increased elasticity of the arteries that helps blood distribution.

The benefits from aerobic training can be significant for both health and athlete client groups. The general public is aware that physical training is beneficial in a general way; knowledge of this kind helps to specify benefits more precisely. Explaining such physiological changes is part of the education process that PTs can provide to clients.

Training for the respiratory system

The following changes are brought about by aerobic endurance training, such as rowing, swimming, and cycling:

- increased exercise ventilation through an increase in lung volume;
- increased VO_2 max;
- increased oxygen uptake at lung tissue/capillary sites;
- decreased ventilation rate during submaximal exercise (ventilation rate is the amount of breaths a person takes in one minute);
- a 'cleaner' respiratory system that results in increased efficiency by utilising more alveoli;
- enhancement of intercostal muscles that help exercise ventilation (intercostals are the muscles that are found between the ribs; they help with breathing, especially during exercise).

Training for the endocrine system

The endocrine system is the physiological system that produces and secretes hormones. These are crucial for maintaining the body in a state of balance (homeostasis). The various hormone-producing organs in the human body will be affected by training sessions. They form an often overlooked system that can be changed through chronic physical exercise. Resistance training in particular increases the synthesis and storage of hormones that contribute to the building and remodelling of muscle tissue. Also, receptors within the neuroendocrine systems will become efficient. An effect of these adaptations is that the number of hormones needed to perform their functions decreases, thereby increasing the efficiency of the whole system.

For hypertrophy clients, the fact that anabolic hormones (including the growth hormones testosterone and insulin) increase after acute and chronic resistance activity can be useful in training. Hypertrophy clients may also be interested to know that training produces more effective use of catabolic hormone cortisol, thereby reducing catabolic effects (the breaking down of tissue). As long as the programming of exercise is carefully considered, the release of cortisol and catabolism will still occur as part of the process of remodelling tissue, but with a maximal anabolic (i.e. growth) effect.

The hormone changes can also be beneficial to weight-loss clients. Decreased low-density lipoproteins (LDLs) and increased high-density lipoproteins (HDLs) will lead to better utilisation of lipids during rest and exercise. Both of these lipoproteins transport fat in the bloodstream, with HDL being responsible for transporting fat away from the arteries. The effects here can help to reduce blood pressure. It should be added that non-insulin dependent diabetics (NIDDMs) can improve their management of glucose using CV exercise. This is brought about by better regulation of the insulin/glucagon system. If glucose is regulated, the client can lose the NIDDM tag completely – a great achievement.

Reflection 3.2

If you were programming for hypertrophy as a response for your client, what exercises and rep ranges would you choose?

The answer from a muscular standpoint is straightforward. Now consider the role of increasing the amount of anabolic hormones in the workout. Power exercises at least one workout a week will increase the levels of these hormones. (Studies indicate that serum testosterone levels increase during power exercises. See Fleck and Kraemer, 2003, pp96–113 for a detailed discussion on this subject.) It may, for example, be appropriate to include one power exercise before conducting a hypertrophy session. The more dynamic and major muscle group exercises that are performed, the more anabolic hormones will be released.

Training for the skeletal system

Training can also produce benefits for the skeletal system. In particular, impact activity such as running and jogging will stimulate the following adaptations. Resistance training (weight-bearing activity) is also excellent at producing these results:

- increase in bone mineral density (with load-bearing and impact exercise);
- increase in strength of connective tissue that binds the skeletal system (ligaments and tendons);
- decrease in the likelihood of the onset of osteoporosis (a degenerative disease that decreases mineral content in the bones);
- lower risk of bone fractures in later life.

The link between programming and physiology

The above information will help the PT to understand how changing duration, frequency, intensity and modes of training as outlined in Chapter 2 can change the client's physiological systems. A question arising here is over what timescale clients adapt to training. There are two ways to describe effects over time. There are (a) acute and (b) chronic effects. Acute effects are those that occur quickly, either during or just after a session. (An example would be a lowering of blood pressure after CV exercise due to the arteries being more elastic straight after the workout.) Chronic effects occur over a longer period of time and tend to last longer. It is chronic effects that the PT is usually aiming for. The precise duration of the change will obviously depend on the client, and the form and frequency of training.

Reflection 3.3

Having trained hundreds of clients, the changes I have witnessed are many and varied. One example that comes to mind is a male client who initially could not perform body weight chin-ups. I trained this client for three months: within one month he could perform one chin-up; within three months he could perform ten. Though the adaptation had taken three months, his goal was realised and he was extremely pleased, so much so that he continued training towards other goals for a further nine months.

Detraining

Detraining results from the principle of reversibility – that is, if a client discontinues training at any time they will start to experience a loss in the adaptation that was gained during their sessions. The degree of loss will depend on the physical status of the client and the specific physiological variable in question. There is evidence that positive adaptation can often be reduced significantly within one to two weeks. Detraining effects apply to resistance training in the same way as endurance training if weight training is ceased. For an excellent table of detraining changes in strength and power, see Fleck and Kraemer (2003), p244. Generally, the longer the period of detraining, the worse the detraining effects will be. Remember that detraining can also occur when the volume or intensity of training is decreased, even though the client may still be training. Explaining the need to avoid the effects of detraining can be a useful tool for maintaining motivation in your clients.

Note that it can be an athlete's goal at a particular point in a season to detrain a particular aspect of their fitness. A periodised programme for an athlete can decrease the intensity of resistance training at an in-season competition period. Although there is a detraining effect, this can be restricted by careful planning of *maintenance* of a particular variable.

Individual adaptation to training

Clients adapt to training in different ways. Using the same training stimulus with more than one client will elicit different gains. This is another reason why the record forms that you complete for each session are so important. You must look at regular intervals to check that your clients are progressing towards their goals. Physiological adaptation is key to these changes. The particulars that are included on the client tracker will provide a starting point for your programming. The age, gender, training status and physical attributes of your clients will all help to determine the physio-logical changes that are possible.

Reflection 3.4

The many trackers that I have used when training clients have indicated what adaptations may occur. The effect of training on older clients has usually been less pronounced than on younger clients, due to the effects of ageing. When training athlete clients, I have usually found that progression and adaptation occur in small increments. They will have already been in a trained state when starting their programmes with me, so it is not surprising that they exhibit gains more slowly than do sedentary clients.

An important aspect in female clients is the sheer difference in testos-terone levels compared to males. On average, females have approximately 10 per cent of the testosterone of males. When that female client comes to you and says she does not want to look like a female bodybuilder, you can assure her that female bodybuilders have to train hard for many years with a strictly controlled diet to get anywhere near that shape! There is no problem over female clients training with free weights – they will not accidentally turn into body builders!

Learning activities

You can study the acute effects of physical activity fairly readily using heart rate monitors, blood pressure monitors and more complex fitness-testing equipment (see Chapter 8). The more important chronic adaptation will be evident only after many sessions – in some cases after months of personal training. Talk to experienced PTs in order to get a long-term viewpoint as to what changes they have witnessed while training their clients. The great interest in personal training is that each client is different: discussion will provide many different angles on how clients respond to training.

Once you have a medium- to long-term client you will start to notice the adaptations that are occurring. Look back over your client record sheets and try to decide what brought about these changes, what worked and what didn't work so well. This will provide invaluable information with which to programme that client in the future. You need to commit to regular fitness testing of your clients where

Activity 3.2

Using the main categories of age, gender, training status and physical qualities of your clients, research the possible differences that may be evident when training these different client groups. To this end, produce a table with each category in a column. Then list the training modes in rows and complete the possible differences in adaptation. The first category in the sample table below has been completed for you as an example:

	Age	Gender	Training status	Physical qualities
Hypertrophy training	More difficult to achieve in older clients.	Females differ from males owing to lower testosterone levels and lower lean body mass overall.	Long-term resistance-trained clients will respond better due to muscle memory and prior morphological changes.	Clients with predominately type 2 muscle fibres will adapt to hypertrophy training and elicit a greater muscle mass than clients with type 1 fibres.
Power training				
Muscular endurance training				
Aerobic training				

appropriate. Without this regular testing it will be difficult to see progression or to base goals on quantifiable data. Chapter 8 provides details of methods of testing PT clients.

Summary

The physiological adaptations that can occur in your clients are varied and can be complex to study. This chapter has provided a summary of the main changes to physiological systems that PTs can bring about. Without knowledge of this type, a PT's programming will lack direction.

It is important too to remember the holistic nature of physiology: no one physiological system will adapt in isolation. It is also necessary to record and consider individual differences between clients.

Further reading

Any exercise physiology textbook will illustrate the adaptations that occur with the onset of physical training. Probably the most widely used is the text by McArdle, Katch and Katch, which outlines the information well in a format that is easy on the eye. Most of my students opt for McArdle when given a choice and if you only procure one exercise physiology textbook, this is probably the best bet. An alternative is Fox, Bowers and Foss. This book will add to your knowledge as it covers exercise physiology from a slightly different perspective and includes some information on the different adaptations in different client groups.

Fox, E, Bowers, R and Foss, M (1998) *The physiological basis for exercise and sport.* 2nd edition. McGraw-Hill.

McArdle, W, Katch, F and Katch, V (2006) *Exercise physiology: energy, nutrition, and human performance.* 6th edition. Lippincott Williams & Wilkins.

Wilmore, J and Costill, D (2005) *Physiology of sport and exercise.* 3rd edition. Human Kinetics.

www.brianmac.co.uk/physiol.htm – a good starting point.

www.asep.org/journals/JEPonline – the *Journal of Exercise Physiology* online.

www.ausport.gov.au/info/topics/physiology.asp – an Australian portal website that will lead you into a wealth of exercise physiology information.

Chapter 4

Nutrition

Within fitness training there is probably no discipline more misunderstood than nutrition. When PTs ask clients about their views on what they eat, what they think they should be eating and what constitutes healthy eating, they receive a vast range of responses. Part of the PT's job is to educate clients regarding fitness, so it falls to the PT to demystify the relationship between food and exercise.

Most clients naturally ask for some sort of nutritional information. Many will ask about weight loss, though some will ask about weight gain. PTs can provide nutritional advice concerning what to eat, how much to eat and what types of food provide healthy options. However, except when PTs are also qualified dieticians, they should not actually plan clients' meals. It is important for PTs to recognise their limitations – and to avoid the risk of being sued!

PTs require a basic understanding of food groups and how issues of nutrition relate to personal training sessions. This chapter is designed to help you to:

1. distinguish the three major food groups and understand their functions;
2. include water, vitamins and minerals in your knowledge base;
3. be aware that there are recommended daily allowances for food;
4. be able to disseminate knowledge regarding weight loss and weight gain;
5. acquire an introductory knowledge of nutritional supplements and their uses.

The major food groups

The three major food groups are carbohydrate, lipids (commonly referred to as fats) and protein. These are also known as 'macronutrients'. In contrast, 'micronutrients' (vitamins and minerals) are so called because they are only needed by the body in tiny amounts.

Carbohydrates

In 'PT-speak', carbohydrates are often known as 'carbs' (or as sugar, though not always in the conventional sense). There is a distinction to be made between simple and complex carbohydrates. Examples of simple carbohydrates include the sugar that you use in hot drinks and the glucose that you find in chocolate bars. These carbohydrates will be digested and absorbed into the bloodstream very quickly, in a few minutes in some cases. They are sometimes termed a 'sugar high'. Examples of relatively complex carbohydrates include rice, pasta and potatoes. Such starchy foods are called complex because they are composed of longer chains of sugars.

The glycemic index

The glycemic index (GI) is a system that ranks foods based on the rate at which ingested food will increase blood sugar levels. Unfortunately, it is not a case of all simple carbohydrates ranking high on the index and all complex carbohydrates ranking low. For example, if we look at different types of sugars, fructose has a low glycemic index of around 20, sucrose has a medium glycemic index of around 70 and glucose has a high glycemic index of 100. Also, variables can affect the GI of a particular food, such as the method of processing or cooking.

High GI carbohydrates are best to ingest during exercise (if applicable) or within a couple of hours after exercise in order to replenish glucose that has been used to fuel the body during the session. Lower GI carbohydrates are generally better to consume before exercise as release is more controlled and so there will be a steady flow of glucose into the bloodstream. Thus, eating lower GI carbohydrates should have an effect on performance during the session. This is why, for example, footballers sometimes eat bowls of pasta a few hours before a game: it increases their energy stores.

As GI values of foods vary, different GI tables provide slightly different scores. However, each GI table is useful for comparing the relative values of foods. The table below (adapted from Clark, 2003) provides a starting point for discussing GI with your clients.

Food	GI value
Glucose	100
Baked potato	85
Jelly beans	78
White bread	73
Brown bread	71
Sugar	68
Mars bar	65
Sweet potato	59
White rice	56
Brown rice	55
Pasta	44
Apple	38
Skimmed milk	32
Grapefruit	25

Search the Internet for different glycemic index tables. Seek trustworthy, scientifically reputable sites providing evidence based on peer-reviewed research (that is, where one scientist's research has been reviewed by other scientists). One good starting point is www.glycemicindex.com/, run by Sydney University. Another is **www.brist.plus.com/dietgi.htm**. This site is run by Bristol Diabetes. Note that organisations concerned with diabetes provide such information because the regulation of blood glucose is vitally important to homeostasis in the human body. Diabetics are unable to regulate this blood glucose properly as the balance of the hormones glucagon and insulin are not maintained. Insulin will increase storage of glucose as glycogen and glucagon will trigger the release of glucose into the bloodstream. This is why diabetics regularly need to check their blood glucose levels using a hand-held machine into which they put a small blood sample. If their blood glucose is too high, then insulin-dependent diabetics will need to inject the required insulin direct into their bloodstream.

Lipids

Found in meat, oils, dairy and some fruit and vegetables, fat is a much misunderstood food group. For example, contrary to popular belief, cholesterol is not all 'bad': note that it serves as a constituent of some hormones and cell membranes among other roles. Different lipids form slightly different chemical components in the human body. The most common are stored as triglycerides. Due to their chemical structure, lipids are not water soluble. (Think about how animal fat floats when it is added to water.) If the lipid is saturated, it will more likely be solid at room temperature.

An example of a saturated fat is lard (animal fat). This can be stored in the body after consumption fairly easily. In contrast, clients will also have heard (from advertisements for margarine) of 'polyunsaturated' fat. Polyunsaturated fat has fewer hydrogen bonds along its carbon chain and is therefore supposedly better for clients to eat – though it is important that the margarine is not made with hydrogenated vegetable oil, as this poses further health risks by affecting the levels of high-density lipoproteins and low-density lipoproteins (both of which concepts are explained below).

Lipoproteins and cholesterol

How can excess saturated fats and excess cholesterol be harmful to clients? The key concept here is atherosclerosis. This refers to the clogging of coronary and main arteries and arterioles, a state that can lead to strokes, myocardial infarction (heart attacks) and angina.

It can be useful to recommend clients to have a blood cholesterol test at their GP surgery. The test will usually measure three factors: total cholesterol levels, HDL (high-density lipoprotein (HDL) and low-density lipoprotein (LDL). HDL is 'good' lipoprotein in the sense that it improves the transport of cholesterol away from the arteries. LDL is 'bad' lipoprotein: it transports the cholesterol towards the arterial wall. The good news for PT clients is that regular exercise will increase HDL levels and decrease overall cholesterol levels.

Some PTs perform cholesterol testing as a service to their clients. Beware of offering this service as it is classed as invasive: it is necessary to break the client's skin in order to obtain a small blood sample. If *any* disease were communicated to the client's blood as a result, the PT could be held liable. It is safer to refer the clients for testing to their GP or to a private health facility.

Carbohydrates and lipids

Carbohydrates and lipids are the preferred fuels for human beings. In exercise the predominant fuel for the first 20 minutes of continuous activity is carbohydrates. After that, lipid utilisation will take over, though not completely. The client will still be utilising carbohydrates as well as lipids beyond 20 minutes because the aerobic energy systems (explained in Chapter 3) rely on lipids to be used in *conjunction* with carbohydrates.

This is where one of the fallacies concerning exercise energy expenditure is to be found. You may have noticed that some cardiovascular machines have training heart rate zone diagrams on them. These supposedly inform the client as to what 'zone' they are working in. One of these zones is termed 'fat burning' and is at the lower end of the zones. As a result, the client is likely to believe that if they work out at a low to moderate intensity, they will 'burn' more fat in the same time frame. This is incorrect: what matters most is the total energy expenditure and the lipid utilisation for a whole session, and this is far more dependent on intensity.

Consider the following cases:

- Session 1: the client works at 130 BPM continuously for 20 minutes. The percentage of lipid utilisation in this session is 30 per cent of the overall energy expenditure, which is 180 kcal. This would mean that the overall lipid utilisation is 54 kcal.
- Session 2: the same client works out at an average of 155 BPM in an interval training session for a total of 20 minutes. The percentage of lipid utilisation in this session is 22 per cent of the overall energy expenditure, which is 280 kcal. This would mean that the overall lipid utilisation is 62 kcal.

Although in the first session the percentage of lipid utilisation is indeed higher (as the diagrams on CV machines would indicate), the second session elicited both a greater energy expenditure and greater lipid utilisation. This was due entirely to the higher intensity, rather than time spent in the 'fat-burning zone'. Clients often need to be educated on the benefits of higher intensity training for weight control.

Each food group has a kcal value for 1 gram of that substance. Typical values are:

- carbohydrate = 4 kcal;
- protein = 4 kcal;
- alcohol = 7 kcal;
- lipids = 9 kcal.

These figures show that lipids are the most energy-dense food group. Due to their structure, lipids are easier for the human body to store. Thus, lipids need to be controlled within clients' diets, especially those with weight and fat loss goals.

Gluconeogenesis

Eating more carbohydrates can be beneficial when seeking to reduce intake of lipids – but only if the total carbohydrate intake is controlled. If the client eats too many calories, they will put on weight, even if those calories are in the form of carbohydrates. The human body can store carbohydrate as lipids and this process is called gluconeogenesis.

Protein

Protein is used by the body for producing and repairing tissue. All musculature and organs are essentially protein, which is made up of amino acids as well as carbon, hydrogen and oxygen. Of the 80 naturally occurring amino acids, only about 20 are used in proteins. The adult human body can synthesise more than half of these, but the remainder (the so-called 'essential amino acids') *have* to be included in the diet or your client may suffer a deficiency.

Meat eaters usually experience no problem gaining amino acids when the protein is digested and absorbed. Meat is a primary source of protein, for obvious reasons (after all, most meat is, in fact, the muscle of an animal or fish). Vegetarian or vegan clients need to manage their diets to include essential amino acids, which can be found, for example, in legumes, nuts and grains. These client groups need to ensure a sufficient supply of amino acids. One resource to help them is the website provided by North Dakota State University at: **www.ag.ndsu.edu/pubs/yf/foods/he463w.htm**.

Protein bars and drinks

If maximum protein utilisation in the body is around 2 grams per kilogram body weight, then a 70 kg elite male athlete would require approximately 140 g of protein per day. That is equivalent to the protein found in one large chicken breast. It is fairly easy for a meat eater to achieve that intake each day. Now if a protein drink and/or bar were added to this diet, what do you think the result will be?

Once the protein needed by the body for repair and growth of tissue has been used, the excess protein will be broken down, with the nitrogen being urinated out and the remaining constituents used as energy or stored as body fat (in the same way as gluconeogenesis). Although moderately higher intakes of protein are rarely harmful, clients using protein products may be literally urinating money away! It is useful to provide clients with a guide to protein intake based on a scale running from 0.8 g per kg body weight for a sedentary individual to a maximum of 2 g per kg body weight for an elite athlete.

Activity 4.2

Work out the approximate protein requirements for the following clients:

1. Justin, who works out three times per week and weighs 68 kg.
2. Abigail, who is an elite weightlifter, trains six times per week and weighs 62 kg.
3. Leon, who is sedentary and weighs 80 kg.

Research the constituents of protein supplements. Work out the amount of protein per serving and add this figure to a meat-eating client's intake. Note the risk of excess that may be evident when clients take protein supplements.

Vitamins, minerals and water

Vitamins

There is no calorific value in vitamins: you cannot take vitamin pills and gain kcal intake. Vitamins are needed in the diet because they cannot be synthesised by the human body. They are found in most foods, especially complex carbohydrates, meat, fruit and vegetables.

There are two classes of vitamins: (a) water soluble and (b) lipid soluble. The water-soluble vitamins are C, niacin and the B complex vitamins. Excess intake of these can be easily excreted through urine. These vitamins are transported in water-based solutions throughout the body and have wide-ranging effects, from the formation of collagen (by vitamin C) to glycogen breakdown (by vitamin B_6).

Lipid-soluble vitamins are A, D, K and E. They are transported by fat. Excessive intake can be more problematic: they will be stored in fatty tissues and are more difficult for the body to dispose of. A and D vitamins can be particularly harmful, causing skin problems and kidney damage respectively. So long as clients have a healthy balanced diet, vitamin intake should not be a problem. If clients want to take vitamin supplements, this is unlikely to cause problems – the concentration of vitamins in pills is carefully managed by the companies that produce them.

A client may ask whether taking vitamins will lead to a better performance in training sessions. The short answer is no, unless the client is actually vitamin deficient. If there is a risk of seriously exceeding the recommended daily allowance (RDA) of a particular vitamin, the client should be referred immediately to a GP.

Minerals

These are used in the production of certain tissues of the body. Bone, nails and teeth need calcium in the diet, while haemoglobin in red blood cells requires iron. If there is a deficiency in one or more minerals, this can cause health problems. Osteoporosis can result from a reduction of calcium intake – especially in the case of young women when their bones are forming and strengthening. This is why dairy products such as milk are an important dietary component.

It is fairly common to come across a client who is anaemic (that is, suffering from an iron deficiency). Iron is important to the oxygen-carrying capacity of your client's blood. Clients suspected of being anaemic should be referred to their doctor for a blood test. This will show whether they require iron supplements. Potential signs of anaemia are low energy levels, a pale complexion and repeatedly feeling faint.

You may well have experienced muscle cramps during intense physical activity. One cause may be a lack of sodium in the body. As sodium contributes to muscle contraction via the nervous activation of the muscle, this is thought to contribute to the cramping seen, for example, towards the end of a 90-minute football match: sodium may be lost during the match through sweating. This explains why sports drinks have a sodium constituent.

Finally, the reader should note that there are many additional roles for vitamins and minerals that are not listed here. The books recommended at the end of this chapter will provide further guidance.

Water

Water makes up to 60 per cent of the body and is vital to health. The human body can only survive a few days without water and clients can quickly become dehydrated if water intake is not properly managed during sessions. Daily recommendations of water intake vary. The British Dietetic Association recommends 2.5 litres per day, of which 1.8 litres should be fluid (the other 0.7 litres coming from water contained in food). Obviously the loss of body water is heightened during exercise as water is a by-product of aerobic metabolism and will be lost through sweat and through water vapour from the mouth.

As water has many functions in the body, including the provision of fluid component of cells and thermoregulation, the dangers of dehydration are not simply a decrease in performance. A client could suffer heat cramps, heat exhaustion or, much worse, heat stroke (which may be life threatening). It is important to ensure that a client is able take regular water breaks throughout their workouts, especially when exercising in a hot and/or humid environment.

The efficacy of sports drinks

There have been many claims by sports drinks manufacturers about the performance-enhancing effects of their products. It is important to remember that simply drinking water may improve performance. It is true, however, that sports drinks contain electrolytes which replace sodium lost through sweating: this helps to maintain the electrolyte balance needed in the body. Some sports drinks contain carbohydrates that will help energy provision in longer duration events. Clients may simply find sports drinks more palatable than water.

Weight loss and weight gain

While many clients have weight loss as a goal, some – especially those who are training for particular sports or bodybuilding – may be seeking weight gain. The topics of weight loss and weight gain are subject to much public misunderstanding, some of it stimulated by the promotion of commercial weight loss programmes. There is a saying in fitness circles that if one of these weight loss products worked the way they are claimed to, the company that produced it would corner a very lucrative market!

The most important point concerning weight loss and gain is, in fact, very simple. Consider Figure 4.1 which shows a set of scales. In other words, if one eats more calories than one expends, one will tend to put on weight, and if one eats fewer calories than one consumes, one tends to lose weight.

The only method of energy intake is through the consumption of food and drink. There are, however, four ways in which the body can expend energy:

- the basal metabolic rate (BMR): the total calories required by the body to maintain its current mass without any movement (usually the largest component of energy expenditure);
- the thermic effect of exercise (TEE), which can be manipulated within training sessions;
- the thermic effect of food (TEF): the body expends calories digesting and absorbing nutrients;
- the thermic effect of disease (TED), which PTs will not want to promote!

Figure 4.1: Energy intake versus energy output scales

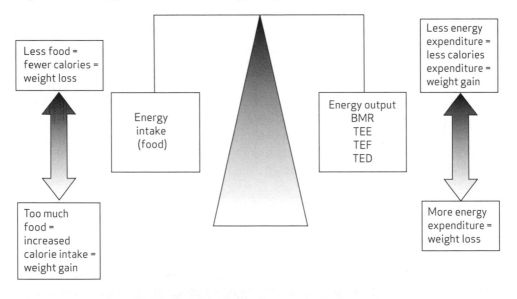

Reflection 4.1

PTs do not always realise that the best way to achieve an increase in energy expenditure is by changing a client's BMR, since this usually forms the main method of expending energy. A trainer can change a client's BMR by increasing the lean body mass (LBM), which is (for our purposes) their muscle mass. Consider how this may be achieved through programming repetitions.

If you answered 'hypertrophy', you were right. Now consider weight loss clients. How many of them will train for hypertrophy? They may well baulk at

Though from the point of view of weight change it is the total calorie intake that is important, there is also the question of the best form in which to consume. The aim should be for a balanced, healthy diet. It is helpful here to consider the so-called food pyramid shown below.

Figure 4.2: Food pyramid

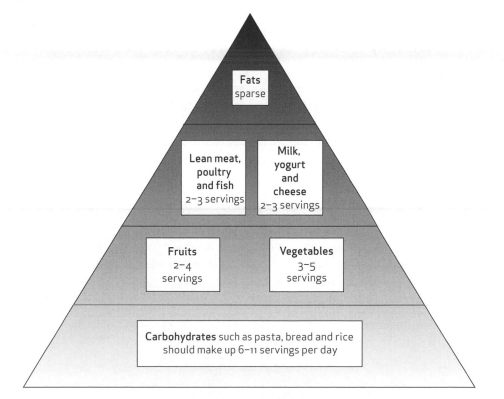

The key point here is that balanced diets are usually the healthiest. Estimates of total RDA vary, but a standard average would be 2,000 kcal for women and 2,500 kcal for men. It is important to remember, however, that individual clients have different requirements. A Tour de France cyclist, for example, will need at least 8,000 kcal per day during competition while a sedentary male who weighs 60 kg will require only around 2,000 kcal.

Reflection 4.2

I have worked with many weight-loss clients and have seen for myself the benefits that result from targeting BMR by increasing LBM. The best results usually come when clients agree to manage their diet as well as training regularly. I have known clients who have tried the Atkins diet, the cabbage diet, the GI diet and many more. The bottom line is that one cannot buck the total calorific expenditure/intake model.

Now ask yourself what you think is a safe lower limit to calorific intake. Clients' daily intakes should not fall more than 500 kcal below their RDA. If they do, their bodies can suffer from the 'yo-yo' diet syndrome. This is where a period of fasting will immediately be followed by the urge to binge eat. This is a natural response of the body and the net result can actually be weight gain. It is better to target a gradual long-term weight loss (say, half a kilogram per week), which is more likely to work.

Rapid weight loss

This is possible only through losing fluid. The process is very different from long-term loss of fat. PTs sometimes encounter 'sweat suit' clients running on the treadmill. The 'suit' makes the client sweat profusely and they will dehydrate very quickly. This should not be common practice because of the dehydration effects discussed above. It is not an advisable method for losing weight (except when controlled for sports performance). If a client arrives wearing a sweat suit, it is important for the PT to educate them about the effects compared to other methods of weight loss.

Weight gain

Now ask yourself what you would do with a client who wants to gain weight. The client may be doing so for aesthetic reasons or to increase LBM for performance purposes. The PT needs to programme two aspects – an increase in the total kcal consumed on a daily basis and a hypertrophy, strength or power resistance programme. The increase in kcal will depend on the client but will often be around 500 per day. Such an increase may require extra meals (or increased portion size) and protein intake towards the higher end of the scale (nearer 2 g per kg body weight).

Food diaries

There are different types of food diaries which can be very useful tools to use with clients. The easiest to use are the '24 recall' and 'weekly portion size' diaries. The

24 recall is exactly that: the client is asked to recall everything they have consumed over the last 24 hours. The information is recorded and used to assess the client's diet.

A superior method is the seven-day weekly portion diary. The PT must sit down with the client and discuss the appropriate portion size for various types of food. With this information in mind, the client keeps a record of everything consumed over a period of seven days. The record can then be analysed using a printed calorie calculator or nutrition software. (Some programmes can also be used to compare energy expenditure with calorific intake.)

Dietary supplements

The use of supplements may be very different from drug abuse, but the PT's moral compass still needs to be in operation. If a PT business sells dietary supplements, it should advocate only those known to be safe and also appropriate for the client. (In fact, most of the good gyms I know do not either sell or provide advice on supplements.) The following points provide a brief guide to the relevant considerations concerning client use of supplements:

1. Creatine: the efficacy of creatine supplements (in the form of creatine monohydrate) is still being researched and the jury is out. Many studies that indicate that creatine supplements, by boosting creatine levels in muscles, may enhance short-burst activities (such as rowing, sprinting and weight-lifting), though only in some participants. The method, temperature and timing of ingestion of creatine supplements are also in question. There is a review of the evidence on the following university website: **www.rice.edu/-jenky/sports/creatine.html**.
2. Caffeine: this is a stimulant that will increase RHR and can make your client more alert. There is some evidence that ingestion by trained athletes can improve the utilisation of lipids over carbohydrates and delay fatigue. The benefits will have to be weighed against the diuretic properties of caffeine, which contribute to dehydration. For a review of the evidence, visit **www.vanderbilt.edu/AnS/psychology/health_psychology/caffeine_sports.htm**.
3. Carbohydrate loading: there is some evidence concerning the benefits. By ingesting larger portions of complex carbohydrates before competition clients may improve performance, especially in longer duration events. For a guide to how to use carbohydrates in a client's diet visit: **http://sportsci.org/news/compeat/grams.html**.
4. L-carnitine: although this substance is known to transport lipids to the mitochondria for energy purposes, there is currently no evidence that supplying extra L-carnitine in a diet will improve this system.
5. Ephedrine: another stimulant that is available in some sports supplements. This substance is banned by the International Olympic Committee and therefore should be viewed with caution. Ephedrine will stimulate heart rate and make the client nervous. The best advice is not to recommend this supplement to your clients.

Other supplements to research are androstenedione, growth hormone releasers, ginseng and amino acid concoctions. Remember that position statements from professional bodies can change over time. It is helpful to visit the following sites: **www.acsmlearning.org/acsm/managepdf.do, www.nsca-lift.org/Publications/ posstatements.shtml** and **www.uksport.gov.uk/assets/File/Generic_Template_ Documents/Drug_Free_Sport/supplements_and_risks_050906.pdf**.

Activity 4.3

Consider what recommendation you would give in the following scenarios:

1. Ellisha wants to lose weight for her wedding in five months' time. She has hired you, has had four successful sessions and seems to working towards her goal. In the fifth session she mentions a TV advertisement she has seen for weight loss pills that say they 'burn body fat without any physical activity' and she is thinking of purchasing a month's supply for £75. How would you respond?
2. Dominic is training for what he calls 'beach protocol' – a slang term meaning he wants to look good on his forthcoming beach holiday. When you started training Dominic for hypertrophy he was already taking a protein drink costing £30 per month. You have advised him that, as a meat eater, he does not need extra protein, though he is welcome to ingest this product as there is little risk. After three months' training three times per week, he approaches you because he 'trusts you' and asks for advice about taking an illegal steroid that he has been offered by a work colleague. What do you advise him to do?
3. Fay has just hired you and is in her initial consultation. She seems to be highly motivated. She then asks about sports supplements. She asks whether there is anything that can help her with her primary goal of decreasing her time for her 10,000 m races she competes in three times per year. Is there any supplement you would recommend and if so, why?

Summary

This chapter has outlined the three major food groups, as well as the micronutrients, especially the main vitamins and minerals. It has also shown that recommended daily intakes of calories may vary but that the central consideration for each client is the balance of calorific intake and expenditure. Finally, the topic of nutritional supplements has been introduced with advice on how to research the topic in detail. Nutrition is a central topic in personal training and one that PTs need to be able to advise clients on, with the support of a knowledge of the underlying science.

Further study

McArdle, W, Katch, F and Katch, V (2006) *Exercise physiology: energy, nutrition, and human performance.* 6th edition. This book contains helpful sections on nutrition applied to sport.

In addition, the following books are recommended.

Clark, N (2003) *Nancy Clark's sports nutrition guidebook.* 3rd edition. Human Kinetics.

Brouns, F (2002) *Essentials of sports nutrition.* 2nd edition. John Wiley & Sons.

McArdle, W, Katch, F and Katch, V (2005) *Sports and exercise nutrition.* 2nd edition. Lippincott Williams & Wilkins.

Maclaren, D (2007) Nutrition and sport: advances in sport and exercise science. Churchill Livingston.

The following websites may prove useful.

www.gssiweb.com/ – this is the official site for the Gatorade Sport Science Institute that includes many sports nutrition articles.

www-rohan.sdsu.edu/dept/coachsci/mastable.htm – this site provides coaching science abstracts on various topics including nutritional supplements.

www.sportsci.org/ – an excellent site for all sport science articles. Follow the link for sport nutrition for related articles.

www.nal.usda.gov/fnic/foodcomp/search/ – a detailed search engine that includes most food groups and their constituent breakdown.

www.coach.ca/eng/nutrition/resources.cfm – some excellent sports nutrition resources are available from this Canadian website.

www.personaltraining1st.com – this site has links to sports supplement companies.

www.bellaonline.com/subjects/7420.asp – some good links to example food diaries that you can try with your clients.

Chapter 5

Motivational psychology

The psychology of personal training forms an interesting aspect of a trainer's working life. Even when working in niche markets, a PT will still encounter many different personalities and client motivations for engaging the services of a PT. Understanding client motivation can help to improve exercise adherence and, indeed, for selling services. A grasp of the psychology of training can help PTs to influence client behaviour.

This chapter is designed to help you to:

1. recognise that every client is psychologically individual;
2. understand that motivational psychology can be used to influence behaviour change;
3. comprehend how exercise adherence can be influenced by PTs;
4. use goal setting in training programmes;
5. apply psychology to business aspects of training.

Each client is an individual. We have already seen that each client is physiologically individual; the same is true psychologically. The factors that need to be taken into account here include:

- personality;
- anxiety;
- motivation.

Personality

One approach to understanding personality is to consider two main types, namely, extroverts and introverts. These types may be viewed on a continuum:

Introvert ———————————————————————————————————▶ Extrovert

Each individual client may be placed at some point on this continuum. The most important time for a PT to ascertain information on a client is during the initial consultation. This provides an opportunity to gain insights into a client's personality while completing a health and lifestyle questionnaire and discussing the client's goals. It may well become apparent during the meeting where, at least approximately, the client stands on the above continuum.

There is no need for personality questionnaires: a client's manner provides plenty of clues. A client who is quiet and difficult to get to open up is probably introverted; one who is lively and talks openly is more likely to be extroverted. It is important that PTs attempt to tailor sessions appropriately, adjusting their own roles according to clients' personalities.

An important factor is the client's self-efficacy. We are concerned here with clients' own impressions of their training abilities. This is affected by their degree of self-confidence. A client's self-efficacy and self-confidence can be influenced by the PT's demeanour. The PT needs to look for opportunities to exert a positive influence.

During training sessions PTs need to be able to assume the following roles:

1. Leader. The PT needs to lead by example, so that the client can follow, and also to convince the client that their advice or instructions will be beneficial.
2. Listener. This role is often overlooked by students. The PT needs to ascertain the client's preferences and wishes so that they can be incorporated into the planning of sessions. This requires the PT both to listen to the client's input and to act upon it.
3. Questioner. Feedback is crucial for ascertaining whether a client is capable of an exercise or whether the intensity is correct. Asking the client is one method of obtaining this information.
4. Motivator. This can be tricky with some clients. The PT needs to try to target each client's primary motivation for training. For example, if a client wants to lose body fat, then the PT can use that motivation to encourage them through an interval session.
5. Training guide. The PT is likely to have greater knowledge than the client of the science of training. The PT is the client's guide to the principles that are applied to training sessions. Such guidance will often need to be subtle and always individualised.
6. Setter of quantifiable goals. The trainer needs to convert the client's aims into goals that are measurable.

The importance of each training role will vary from client to client. The trainer needs to 'read' each client on a session-by-session basis and adjust accordingly. The trainer's persona will need to adjust from client to client. This is *not* to say that trainers should not be themselves; rather, their *manner* will need to vary.

Reflection 5.1

Of the many different client personalities I have encountered as a trainer, there are two who fit particularly clearly into the extrovert/introvert framework. Probably the most extroverted client was a middle-aged American guy who used to fly in to the UK from the US and within a couple of hours

Reflection 5.1 continued

would turn up at the gym in a heightened state of readiness. He would invariably try to get a session without an appointment and when asked what type of session he wanted would always answer, 'Tough!' On most occasions I would administer a boxing workout at a high intensity. The session would be heard throughout the gym. After the session he would shout, 'Great workout!' and be gone as quickly as he'd arrived. Compare this to another client who would turn up at the gym and quietly start a warm-up. I would have to approach the client myself. During the workout this client would quietly perform the exercises I gave him with polite conversation and a friendly handshake at the end. You can imagine that if I had not tailored the two sessions to their personalities there would have been significant problems! The first client expected a loud and intense workout, while the second client would have been embarrassed and confused by this type of treatment.

Activity 5.1

Ask a friend to role-play the part of a prospective client. Arrange a mock initial consultation. Ask them to role-play a client from a certain point on the personality continuum above and try to discern where they think they are on the scale. This dialogue should provide useful practice for conducting consultations in general as well as the psychological aspects. In addition, if you work in a gym, ask to shadow a PT on his or her consultations. During each consultation, try to assess the balance of roles required for training the client.

Anxiety

Many clients will be anxious during the initial sessions and especially during the consultation. This can affect both performance during the sessions and exercise adherence, so the trainer needs where possible to try to reduce client anxiety.

It is helpful at this point to understand that there are two categories of anxiety: 'trait' anxiety and 'state' anxiety. Trait anxiety is found within the client and will manifest itself regardless of the place and time the client finds him- or herself in. Some clients are anxious over any form of training and believe themselves to be ill-equipped to perform physical activity. This type of client provides a particular challenge for the PT. Such clients need reassurance and positive feedback during their sessions.

State anxiety is situation-specific and can manifest itself in different environments. A client may hire your services as the thought of the alternative – group physical activity in a public place – may be abhorrent and create extreme anxiety. A one-to-one session in a 'safe' home environment may be perfect for such a client. Psychological research indicates that anxiety is usually a *combination* of the two states and results in an 'interactional' viewpoint. The PT must try to reduce both forms of anxiety through careful session planning and execution. The overriding direction for the PT to pursue is that of positivity and achievement throughout your sessions as this will naturally reduce anxiety in your client.

Reflection 5.2

One home client that I trained seemed anxious when performing any exercise that required co-ordination. She would say, 'I'm a motor moron when it comes to co-ordination.' I later found out that this state anxiety stemmed from a gym class session that she had attended where the instructor had gone through the session ignoring her inability to perform the routine. I had to reassure her over a number of sessions that she was capable of performing those exercises. I broke each exercise down into parts and let her explore the movement pattern, with only positive feedback being provided by me. Over the course of two months she gained self-efficacy and eventually followed a complete home fitness video full of complex moves!

Motivational psychology

PTs need always to consider clients' motivation. Without motivation clients will not exercise (or continue to hire a PT). Motivation can be either intrinsic or extrinsic. Often the training programme can be designed to appeal to both. Intrinsic motivation is found within the client, as it were: such clients exercise for the love of it and will continue to hire a PT as long as they think they need to. Extrinsic motivation is linked to other rewards – for example, the client may wish to drop a dress size or may have decided to reward themselves with a present if they complete a certain number of sessions. This extrinsic motivation can be used by the PT to create alternative goals that may work as well as intrinsic motivation if chosen carefully. Again, the PT has to 'read' each client to decide what will provide the greatest motivation.

Activity 5.2

How do you discover your client's intrinsic motivation? You need to ascertain your client's 'base values'. Draw up a brief questionnaire that will provide an answer. Questions could include general background motivational questions, such as what their top priorities are in their life. Include specific fitness questions also, such as what the client wants out of their sessions. Try the questionnaire out on a colleague. Now see how you can link sessions to the client's answers. It is surprising what links you can create! For example, a client may identify as a priority that they want to enjoy the free time they have with their young family. You can link this easily into the training sessions: training enables increased energy and fitness for enjoying time with their children now and in the future. Overall, the questionnaire can help you to form links with the client's own reasons for behavioural change and their motivations.

Reflection 5.3

I have trained the wedding client who wants to fit into a smaller dress size on her special day, as well as clients whose main motivation is to reduce their blood pressure and improve their overall health. I firmly believe that if some of these clients did not have such motivation, then they would not train. Sometimes I am surprised by a client's motivation for hiring me. The most surprising motivation that I have heard of came from a client who wanted to treat themselves to a new car and allied this to a goal to lose 2 stones in weight. When they lost the weight, they bought the new car and discontinued their training sessions! I have seen two 'city types' who were extremely competitive with each other and this was very evident in their sessions. On one occasion I was stretching one of them and my trainer colleague happened to be stretching the other. The clients then persisted to get us to stretch their hamstrings to see which one was more flexible. Clearly their motivation was based on competition and the desire to establish superiority.

Motivation: trait and state

Just as anxiety motivation can be either trait or state in nature, so too can motivation. You will probably have heard of 'well-motivated' clients who will be highly motivated *regardless* of the activity asked of them. Such clients will have high trait motivation. Some clients, on the other hand, will perform well in a class or group environment, but then lose motivation when on their own. Such clients demonstrate *state* motivation. They probably need a social aspect to their training. There is also an interactional viewpoint where clients have a degree of both types of motivation.

A PT can affect motivation by considering both trait and state motivation when training clients. In particular, motivation for training needs to be taken into account in goal setting. One-to-one sessions provide a huge benefit here, enabling the PT to create individualised programmes and focus on client motivation.

The following is a list of some typical general motivations for performing physical activity:

1. **Aesthetic**. This concerns clients' perception of how they look. This is not to be confused with how they *actually* look! Perception and reality can be very different. Most clients will have an aesthetic motive at least to some extent.
2. **Weight loss**. This is very common in the health client group. The PT needs to extol the virtues of fat loss rather than just weight loss. This is where fitness testing skills come to the fore: they provide body fat data at regular intervals in the client's programme and can act as a powerful motivator.
3. **Physical health**. With GP referral clients (see Chapter 11) this will be the primary goal. The aim could be to reduce blood pressure, de-stress, manage diabetes or provide rehabilitation from injury.
4. **Performance**. This is the athlete client group's primary goal. Examples of aims include increasing VO_2 max, reducing personal best times, increasing weight lifted or improving team-sport agility.

5. **Psychological health**. This is often either missed or underestimated by personal trainers. There have been many studies that point to the psychological benefits of exercise. A good start for researching this area is Penedo and Dahn's (2005) article 'Exercise and well-being: a review of mental and physical health benefits associated with physical activity' in the journal *Current Opinion in Psychiatry*.
6. **Enjoyment**. This is an intrinsic motivator. There are some clients who train purely for the enjoyment of being physically active. They often respond to the fact that PT sessions are dedicated time for themselves.
7. **Competition**. This can be the case even if the client is not an athlete. Clients with a competitive nature may be trying to beat themselves or have goals related to their friends or colleagues.
8. **Social**. Some clients appreciate the opportunity to talk to someone who is not associated with them more personally. If they train in groups they may value the sessions as part of their social life.

A client may have multiple motives for entering into exercise. The first four motives on the above list are likely to apply to the majority of the clients you will train.

It is useful for PTs to have a grasp of the main theories that seek to explain clients' motivations for exercising. One theory that is particularly useful is **need achievement theory** (NAT). NAT considers the relation between a person's personality and the situation that he or she is in. It involves a consideration of the client personality through focusing on what the client *needs to achieve* relative to their *need to avoid failure*. Combined with the situation in which the client finds him- or herself, these needs produce a 'resultant tendency' which, when combined with the client's emotional state (e.g. pride or shame), will determine success or failure when performing in sessions. For example, a client with a lack of a need to achieve a lowering of blood pressure, combined with a dislike for physical activity and an overall low self-esteem, is unlikely even to make the decision to start the programme in the first place.

A second useful theory is **achievement goal theory** (AGT). This theory is designed to help ascertain clients' motivation through focusing on their desire to complete their goals, their belief in their ability to achieve, and their achievement behaviour (e.g. commitment and degree of focus). It is the relationship between the nature of the client's goals and their belief that they are capable of achieving them which can determine whether the achievement behaviour will be evident. For instance, a client who demonstrates a strong desire to complete a goal of running a marathon in less than three hours, combined with an unshakeable belief that this is possible and with a commitment to training, will have a good chance of succeeding. Positive feedback on performance in relation to goals can be effective here. Where there is negative feedback to be imparted, the PT can use the 'sandwich method', i.e. placing the negative feedback comment in between two positive comments ('You performed the squat well with regard to the positioning of the bar. You could have gone a little deeper with your thighs, but overall it was a good attempt.'). The PT needs to provide ability-centred feedback and *not* attribute success to luck or the fact that an exercise was easy. It is important above all to ensure that feedback is honest, so that it does not come back to haunt the PT in the light of fitness-testing results.

Goal setting

Goals are useful both for the client and the trainer. Though the client's goals may be subjective, the trainer needs to convert them into objective ones. There are three types of goals: outcome, process and performance.

Outcome goals are concerned with competition. For example, there may be an inter-departmental five-a-side football tournament at work that the client wants to win. Process goals relate to stages within the exercise performance. For example, a client who wants to perform handstand presses may have a goal to keep his or her back straight in order to allow the proper execution of this exercise. Performance goals are specified irrespective of competitors. For example, a client may wish to row 2,000 m on an indoor rowing machine in under eight minutes. With each client it is important to decide which goals to prioritise. The PT can do this by using primary, secondary and tertiary goal setting.

Activity 5.3

Janice is a client who tells you in her consultation that she wants to lose weight, improve her fitness, and 'look like Madonna'. Her primary trainer goal will be to lose a certain percentage of body fat. Her secondary goal will be to increase her VO_2 max to a specified level. While her first two goals may easily be converted into trainer goals, the tertiary goal may be more of a challenge. You can discuss aspects of Madonna's 'look' and work towards the leanness that she exhibits through the client's primary goal.

Now consider what trainer goals might be appropriate for clients who have the following goals:

- Paul wants to 'look like David Beckham' and is currently overweight and unfit.
- Danielle wants to be able to move like Lara Croft (as in the film *Tomb Raider*). She is currently inflexible and relatively unfit.
- Patricia would like to put on muscle mass and maybe start to compete as an amateur bodybuilder. She is an ectomorph and finds putting on muscle mass a hard task.

Recommendations for goal setting

Goals need to be challenging, but attainable. Unattainable goals demotivate clients in the long run. All goals should be 'SMART', that is:

- S = specific;
- M = measurable;
- A = achievable;
- R = recordable;
- T = timed.

Note that the need for goals to be 'timed' can relate to various timescales – short, medium, and long. Generally, short-term goals should be achievable within one month, medium-term goals within six months and long-term goals between six months to a year. Do not rely purely on long-term goals: clients are likely to lose interest.

Goal setting needs to grow out of needs analysis and once again the initial consultation provides an excellent opportunity to begin this process. The client must have their wishes respected when goal setting. Unless the client 'buys into' the programme there will be significant motivational problems. Once the PT has converted the client goals into trainer goals, adherence can be increased through the use of an agreement with the client based on the goals. Research has shown that the use of these tools can increase motivation in some client groups. The document will detail the commitment needed by your client to achieve the goals that have been agreed. By signing this agreement the client is 'promising' to deliver. Of course, if the client does not deliver, the agreement will need to be adjusted in due course. This is quite separate from any commercial contract you may have with the client.

Before each session the PT should check with the client which aspects of their goals they wish to work on. The client is paying for the service and will feel empowered by being asked for an opinion. It is important, though, to avoid training for only one aspect of a client's goals within sessions, unless the PT can be sure that the client is working on the other aspects outside sessions.

Reflection 5.4

I had a male client whose primary goal was to increase hypertrophy of his musculature. When it came to the sessions, he asked only for 'chest and bicep' workouts. I initially trained him according to his wishes with the proviso that he completed back, leg and shoulder exercises in his own time. It soon became apparent that this was not happening at all, so I sat and explained the effects of muscle imbalance. Fortunately, the client took the lesson on board and allowed me to train other muscle groups within his sessions.

The goals that a PT sets for clients need to be implemented at the right time and evaluated on a regular basis to see whether the training programme is working or not. There should be encouragement to achieve their goals throughout sessions and re-adjustment either when goals are met or when it is clear that the client is not making sufficient progress towards them. The process of evaluating progress also needs to be individualised. Over-monitoring can demotivate a client by giving the impression of a lack of progress. Some clients will not react well if their goals are readjusted due to non-achievement. Readjustments need to be discussed subtly.

Another, often overlooked, way to augment goals is to involve a client's 'signifi-cant others' (that is, the people around them who matter most). These people can become powerful allies. An example would be a client's spouse, who can provide excellent motivation to do something that will enhance the prospect of achieving the goal. With GP referral clients, the significant other may be the doctor – though GPs are not always keen to work in partnership with personal trainers, it is a possibility worth exploring.

Activity 5.4

Try to convert the following client goals into trainer goals:

- Paul wants to reduce his blood pressure and stress levels, and be able to run for the bus if he needs to.
- Shelley would like to increase her aerobic fitness for her step class that she attends once per week and drop a dress size by her summer holidays.
- Candice has said that she wants to lose weight for her wedding in nine months and be able to win a tennis match against a work colleague in five months' time.

Carefully consider what types of goals are required. For each client, draw up a draft agreement.

Psychological research has indicated that goal setting works well with many clients. Locke and Latham's study (2002) brings together 35 years of goal setting research and looks at new directions. Strecher (1995) looks at goal setting from a general health perspective.

Exercise adherence and how to increase retention

An application of psychological understanding can benefit both the client, in terms of fitness, and also the trainer in commercial terms. For example, enhanced exercise adherence is in both parties' interests. In general, exercise adherence can be improved by focusing on the client's psychological (as well as physical) make-up; empowering the client through their own goal setting; ensuring that the programme is designed at the correct intensity; and promoting regular exercise. Below are some models that are useful to apply when addressing exercise adherence.

The **health belief** model applies to clients who believe that by exercising they will decrease the likelihood of disease. For them, the benefits of training with a PT outweigh the negative ideas that they may have about PT sessions. It may be that a majority of a PT's clients are of this type. This model is a powerful motivator because it relates directly to life expectancy. If someone genuinely recognises this benefit, then once they have committed to physical activity adherence is likely to be strong. (See, for example, Haase, 2004, a study which examined this model in relation to 19,000 students from 23 countries.)

Social cognitive theory suggests that behaviour change is built on three different sets of factors: environmental, personal and attributes of the behaviour itself. The concept of self-efficacy plays a pivotal role. The client must believe themselves capable of performing the behaviour, must perceive an incentive to do and must value the expected outcomes. Outcomes may have immediate benefits (such as feeling energised following a workout) or long-term ones (e.g. improved health). This approach is thus linked to the client's self-esteem (the value that one places on oneself and one's abilities). Clients with high self-esteem are more likely to believe that they are able to achieve goals and to strive towards making their lives better. Clients who already possess strong self-esteem are more likely to enter into personal training agreements. They often make good clients.

Planned behaviour theory proposes that a 'behaviour intent' is influenced by (a) the client's attitude towards that behaviour, (b) social pressure as perceived by the client, and (c) client perception of how easy or difficult performing the behaviour will be. This model is clearly applicable with clients for whom the perception of themselves by significant others is a key factor. For example, a client's spouse may provide the impetus for the client to seek to become healthier and more energetic. The spouse can be involved in goal setting and act as a 'helper' who can keep an eye on what the client is eating, what exercise he or she is doing, and so on. The danger, of course, is that the client may rebel against what they may see as control or coercive behaviour. For a list of research papers dealing with the planned behaviour model, see **www-unix.oit.umass.edu/~aizen/tpbrefstxt.html**.

Some psychologists believe that the process of exercise adherence is more complex and that it is helpful to consider clients as each being at a particular stage of exercise participation (the **transtheoretical model**). Typical stages are as follows:

1. Pre-contemplation stage – the client has not yet contacted a PT (and may not do so).
2. Contemplation – this is the stage where the PT first comes into contact with a prospective client. The client has made an initial commitment to an exercise programme.
3. Preparation – when the first PT session has been booked.
4. Action – when the PT has trained this client at least once.
5. Maintenance – the client has rebooked for a certain number of sessions (say, ten).
6. Termination – either the client has re-entered the pre-contemplation stage (not exercising) or they have booked the PT in the long term, engraining training into their life.

For a personal training business, the contemplation stage is a very important one. It is useful at this point especially for PTs to use the health benefit model, extolling the benefits of physical activity. PTs can emphasise that regular physical activity will tend to:

*   reduce cardiac disease risk factors;
*   improve skeletal structure;
*   decrease the likelihood of illness;
*   provide weight management;
*   make the client look better;
*   increase self-esteem and confidence.

In addition, it is helpful to explain the ways in which one-to-one training can provide a higher level of service. One barrier that often requires attention is a client's sense of fatigue. A client may believe that they lack the energy required for PT sessions. The point to emphasise here is that an increase in physical activity will actually *improve* energy levels.

Activity 5.5

Draw up a sample 'decision balance sheet' for a prospective client to use when considering whether to hire a PT. You can do this by drawing a large weighing scale in which factors can be 'weighed' by the client. Complete a form yourself to help you to help the client complete theirs. It is amazing the effect that such a sheet can have on clients!

Other methods to increase exercise adherence

A PT can provide cues to exercise. These can include posters, notes or, as previously discussed, support from significant others. Prompts can be verbal – for example, 'I'll book you in for the same time every week then.' If the client has achieved certain goals already, this achievement should be highlighted to help maintain impetus. Prompts may also be symbolic. For example, if a client invests in workout equipment at home, this will keep them thinking about rebooking sessions with the PT.

The use of record forms and client trackers (discussed in Chapter 6) will help to provide reinforcement. Another incentive might be to provide 'free stuff' – for example, branded items or a discount – when a client has achieved a certain threshold. It is also good for PTs to promote the idea that exercise should be conducted for its own sake and for sessions to be made as enjoyable and convenient as possible for the client and with as much client input as possible, thereby helping to grow the client's intrinsic motivation.

Activity 5.6

Develop a points reward system for your clients. Work out how many 'bank of PT' points a client needs to accumulate before they receive something in return. It may be that you relate this to, for example, achievement of goals, number of sessions completed or referral of one of the client's friends.

One final idea that may be applied to the question of exercise adherence is the 'future self' model. This brings together behavioural change, outcome goals and client motivators. The PT discusses with the client a significant change and works with them to achieve a long-term goal to realise a future self. The client will have an idea in their mind's eye as to how they will look and feel when they have met this goal. This is an image of the client's future self. Problems can occur, however, if the client then fails to achieve the future self envisaged, for example, by falling short of one of their training goals. The notion of the future self can be a powerful motivator, but should be used only with those clients who:

will envisage themselves realistically after their goals have been reached (some clients are apt instead to use images of famous people as models for what they want to look like – for example, Brad Pitt in the film *Fight Club*; or

will not be too discouraged if they fail to achieve all their targets (note that it is usually better to set goals on the low side rather than on the high side – if a client outperforms, this is likely to encourage adherence).

Summary

Personal training needs to be individualised for each client. The PT needs to understand a client's motivation and to set appropriate goals. Psychological under-standing can be used to enhance exercise adherence, bringing both health benefits to the client and business benefits to the PT. PTs can help clients to appreciate the value of training programmes and to change their behaviours. It should be added, however, that change must ultimately be self-change: a PT cannot force a client to change!

Further study

ACSM (2007) *ACSM's resources for the personal trainer.* 2nd edition. Lippincott Williams & Wilkins

Baechle, T and Earle, R (2000) *Essentials of strength training and conditioning.* 2nd edition. Human Kinetics

Marcus, B and Forsyth, L (2003) *Motivating people to be physically active.* Human Kinetics.

Weinberg, R and Gould, D (2007) *Foundations of sport and exercise psychology.* 4th edition. Human Kinetics.

www.exrx.net/Psychology/AdherenceTips.html – some general tips on exercise adherence.

http://sportsmedicine.about.com/od/tipsandtricks/a/gettingstarted.htm – more general information on adherence and includes: http://z.about.com/f/p/440/graphics/pdf/en/20000.pdf, a sample sheet to use to try and ascertain your client's motives for exercising.

www.bangor.ac.uk/~pes004/exercise_motivation/scales.htm – for those interested in researching the reasons people exercise this will provide an academic starting point.

www.topendsports.com/psychology/motivation-moving.htm – tips you can use with clients on how to 'get moving'.

PART 2

Practice

Chapter 6

Session planning and recording

In order to achieve clients' goals, PTs need to ensure that every session is properly planned. Each session requires goals based on the client's overall programme, and the client's progress towards those goals needs to be carefully recorded and reviewed. Each detail of each session contributes to the fabric of the client's achievements. This chapter outlines four key components: client trackers, record keeping, self-evaluation and professionalism. In addition, the chapter signposts the code of conduct advocated by the Register of Exercise Professionals for the United Kingdom (REPs).

Conducting one-to-one personal training sessions requires many different skills. The ways in which two different trainers might train the same client can vary hugely. The self-evaluation scheme given in this chapter provides a tool for you to use to examine the appropriateness of various approaches.

This chapter is designed to help you to:

1. plan training sessions;
2. understand the need to keep medically related records;
3. be able to record an array of workouts;
4. evaluate sessions;
5. recognise the need for PTs to be professional at all times.

Introduction to planning

Personal training session planning and recording should be viewed as a cyclical process. A PT will plan a session based on the goals of a client; administer the session; record the session; evaluate the session and then review the programme, and plan the next session. It is helpful, then, to see this process as a cycle (see Figure 6.1).

Taking a professional approach of this type has two benefits: it improves the quality of service for the client and it enhances the PT's own professional development. In outlining PTs' professional practice, this chapter will cover a number of timescales from short-term, session-by-session issues, to long-term developmental issues.

Figure 6.1: Cycle of session planning

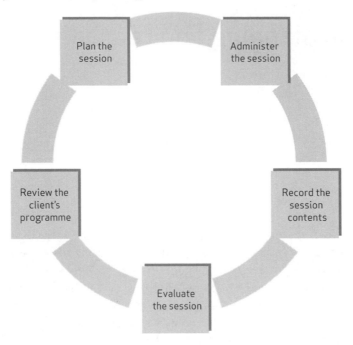

The single most important point when planning sessions is to keep asking 'why'? A PT should ask this question about every aspect of every session. For example:

- 'Why did I choose those exercises?'
- 'Why did I put them in that order?'
- 'Why did I take the client's pulse at that point in the workout?'
- 'Why did I stretch those muscles?' – and so on.

It is often said in personal training that 'you're only as good as your last session'. It does not matter if you trained your client perfectly in a session last month; *every* session should be as good as possible. PTs need to examine their practice critically and always to be able to justify – to themselves and their peers – the decisions taken over each session. A PT needs to ask at each stage of a session, 'Would this stand up to professional scrutiny?'

In part, this is a question of ensuring that sessions are based on scientific understanding, as discussed elsewhere in this book. It is also a question of how the client is managed. In the UK, the REPs code of conduct covers most eventualities. You are strongly recommended to read and adhere to this code. The document, which is available at **www.exerciseregister.org/InfoDocs.htm**, covers questions of rights, relationships, personal responsibilities and professional standards.

A PT needs to be attentive to the client at all times during the session. The client is paying for the PT to train them, not to be distracted by extraneous stimuli! A PT has a duty of care for each client during each session; this means that the PT is responsible for the reasonable safety of the client *and* the quality of training at all times.

At this point you may well be thinking, 'What happens if things do go wrong? A PT cannot be expected to be *totally* responsible for every client action!' Suppose, for example, a client ignores the PT's advice and attempts a lift that the client is not capable of. Is the PT liable for negligence? It is in order to cover such events that every PT needs to take out insurance. A PT *must* be insured. Third-party liability policies often provide cover of up to £2 million and some provide more than that. This provides protection to the PT in the event of a client suing them.

Reflection 6.1

Most trainers look after their clients attentively. On the other hand, I have witnessed trainers arriving late, answering mobile phone calls during a session, or wandering off to chat to colleagues! I also remember one trainer training a client at far too high an intensity. The client was overweight and not able to complete the exercise he was doing at the time, let alone what the trainer asked him to do subsequently. The client looked nauseous and unhappy. Apart from the fact that the trainer probably lost that client, the situation was dangerous as the client was obviously training anaerobically. Luckily for the trainer, he was not part of my team, otherwise he would have found himself in severe trouble!

Attentiveness during a session can take many forms. A polite greeting and 'goodbye' are, of course, essential. Taking perceptual signs (heart rates and RPE) also forms part of the trainer's focus on the client. In addition, a PT needs to consider questions of timing, such as when to provide a workout towel, when to allow water breaks and when to provide feedback to the client. Each session will require different answers to these questions, so the PT needs to be able to work 'on the fly', reacting to each session as it progresses. Overall, it is commitment to the client that lies at the heart of successful personal training.

The tracker

The client tracker is a tool that allows trainers to view the record of any client on one side of A4 paper. The information included on the tracker will cover the health status of the client, training programme and test results. The record needs to cover the background and the workouts of the client. Trackers enable PTs to keep health- or medical-related records – something very few trainers manage to do. Two examples of trackers are provided at the end of this chapter. One is a blank version with headings explained and the other is a sample of a completed tracker showing how recorded information looks. In addition, an *Excel* worksheet version is freely downloadable from **www.personaltraining1st.com**.

Each client should have a separate file containing an up-to-date tracker and copies of charted workouts. In theory, by having this information to hand, any competent trainer would be able to train any client with little further background research. Trackers also allow information to be updated as and when a client's training or health status changes.

The method used for filing matters as PTs are responsible for keeping sensitive information regarding clients. Cardboard folders work well for this purpose: the tracker may be stapled to the inside of the folder with updated sheets attached as needed. The client's name may be written on the outside of the folder, which should then be filed alphabetically. It is advisable to keep the files in a locked metal filing cabinet. A client's billing information can be kept in this file for added security. An alternative is to use palm-held computers. These allow the files to be recorded electronically while training the client and then saved with an electronic version of the tracker that can be updated instantly. This has the advantage of saving paper and filing space, but again, careful attention must be paid to security issues if you use this method.

> ### Reflection 6.2
>
> *When I have witnessed PT sessions without any recording sheets in use, I have always wondered how the PT can expect to remember all of the relevant information. Some trainers seem merely to work on an exercise-by-exercise basis without any real plan or even any detailed knowledge of what they did with clients before the current workout. Or, worse, a client may turn up with a change in their status and the PT may not know or bother to find out!*

Recording workouts

Whereas the tracker is invaluable for the 'big picture', the PT also needs a method of recording each PT session. It is helpful to look at the example of the completed record sheet to be found on p83. Note that in the top left-hand corner it gives the client's name, target heart rate zone and body weight. Each sheet contains a record of three workouts. For each session there is a record of:

- the date;
- the client's feelings;
- the PT's observations;
- the aim of the session;
- the session number;
- the main body of the workout (recorded in a shorthand notation);
- additional notes.

Though it is not easy to make records of a workout while it is in progress, this is a skill that can be learnt. It is important to do so, as it is all too easy to forget details of a session once it has finished. At the end, the record of each session should be signed by the PT.

These sheets provide an invaluable resource for the PT. Ideally, they will provide evidence of progression over time. They will certainly help the trainer to review the programme. If, for example, a PT has trained a client for three months and has 12 completed sessions on your record forms, this will provide information on, for example, intensity at different workloads on CV equipment and weight lifted for RMs during resistance activity. If, say, a client has increased a lift by 10 per cent over three months, it may be appropriate to set an additional 10 per cent as a goal for the next three months. Sharing such information with the client is an excellent way to provide motivation. If the client knows that the PT is recording each workout, it shows that the PT is professional and interested in the client's progression.

Activity 6.1

Jonathon has been training with you for one month. In that time he lifted 60 kg for 10 RM chest press, 80 kg for 10 RM leg press and 30 kg for 10 RM for shoulder press. How would you assess what increases of each of these weights to implement over the next month of training?

Planning training sessions

The detail that a PT includes in the main body of a session will vary, as every session will be different in some manner. The schedule for an hour session might be:

1. complete the first five sections of the record sheet;
2. warm-up (minimum 4 minutes);
3. if necessary perform a passive stretch on the client;
4. the main body (approximately 40 minutes in an hour session);
5. cool-down (minimum 3 minutes);
6. perform a passive stretch on the client (approximately 5 minutes);
7. complete record form and sign off.

It is important to ensure a punctual start and then to monitor the running time so as not to overrun.

Shorthand notation for records

During the workout it can be difficult to keep up with the recording of the exercises. You may well be wondering, 'How does a PT maintain these records at the same time as thinking about the next exercise?' One tool that helps is learning trainer shorthand. This gives the PT the ability to write fast and record in detail. Examples of trainer shorthand are given in the tables on p74.

You can adapt the shorthand to include other exercises. Each gym has particular kinds of CV and resistance equipment. These may be differentiated by adding an initial – for example, a 'finesse machine' calf raise could be represented by 'FCR'.

Exercises

CP	Chest press	DL	Dead lift	SROW	Seated row
LP	Leg press	SN	Snatch	LADD	Leg adduction
LPD	Lat pulldown	CL	Cleans	LABD	Leg abduction
SP	Shoulder press	PP	Push press	STUPS	Step-ups on a bench
LE	Leg extension	POP	Power pull	BC	Bicep curl
LC	Leg curl	PUPS	Press-ups	TE	Tricep extension
LR	Lateral raise	ABS	Abdominals	T BAR	T bar row
FR	Front raise	SQ	Squat	INT ROT	Internal rotation
BOR	Bent-over row	CR	Calf raise	EXT ROT	External rotation
OAR	One-arm row	SCR	Seated calf raise	TIB ANT	Tibialis anterior

Equipment

BB	Barbell	MED	Medicine ball	ROPE	Skipping rope
OBB	Olympic barbell	●	Gym (Swiss) ball	BAND	Resistance band
DB	Dumb-bell	EZ BAR	EZ barbell	BBar	Body bar
ROW	Rowing	X trainer	Cross trainer	BIKE	Gym cycle
TM	Treadmill	STEP	Stepper	SPIN	Spin bike

Modifications/others

DEC	Decline	ISO	Isometric	WG	Wide grip
INC	Incline	♥	Heart rate	ALT	Alternate grip
JUMP	Jumping	⑨	RPE (number in circle)	10x12x3	Weight x reps x sets
DY	Dynamic	CG	Close grip	STR	Stretch

Self-evaluation

Once the first few record forms have been completed, the PT is in a good position to self-evaluate. Workout sessions may be divided into 12 separate areas. The PT can award him- or herself a mark out of 10 for each section. Where possible, another trainer may be used to provide evaluation marks instead. Here is a suggested format for a scoresheet.

Component	Best practice	Score /10
The warm-up	This should be around 5 minutes, performed relative to the client's goals, low THRZ, appropriate to the tracker. HR/RPE should be checked to make sure that a warm-up is occurring.	
Selection of exercises	Appropriate to the aim of the session; equipment available to the trainer; related to the tracker information; consideration taken of client's training status on that day.	
Utilisation and replacement of equipment	Safe replacement of equipment used; equipment used that is specific to the session aims; innovation in usage of the equipment (if applicable).	
Tracker adherence	The trainer must be aware of this during the entire workout, if there is deviation or inappropriate exercises are chosen, you lose marks.	
Recording of the session	Correct shorthand is used and the complete record of the workout is available straight after the end of the session.	
Session is based on science	Everything the trainer prescribes during the session is based on the programming essentials chapter. No fad exercises or bad advice.	
HR and RPE	Should be taken at appropriate times and ideally a minimum of four to five times in the session. This section can also include pre- and post-session BP measurement for hypertensive clients.	
Commitment	How committed to your client were you? You should have been attentive and shown modification of the session where necessary. You should also include pertinent feedback to your client.	
Trainer spotting	Correct placement of you and the client when performing resistance exercises. Observation and intervention by the trainer when necessary (see	

	Chapter 7). Another description of this activity is appropriate 'hands on' by the trainer during the workout.	
Stretching	Performed by the client at some stage during the workout. The trainer would normally perform assisted stretching on the client with appropriate choice and execution of the stretch. This should also be related to the client training notes on the tracker.	
Progression and flow	The workout should flow seamlessly between sections and exercises, without the client 'hanging about' to allow the trainer to record or think about what activity should be completed next. The session should include some progression based on the previous workout, even if it is slight.	
The cool-down	Ideally should be a minimum of three to four minutes and should allow the client to reduce HR to <120 BPM. This should be monitored by the trainer to ensure a safe response has occurred by the client.	
Total		/120

The total score here will be out of 120 possible points. The PT should aim to score over 100 and never to fall below 80. This is not easy, but complacency is unacceptable. (After all, just one dissatisfied customer can be very bad for business!)

If another trainer is used to perform the evaluation, that person should have at least as much experience as the PT being observed, otherwise the scores recorded will have little or no value. The evaluator should also try to remain impartial and totally objective when scoring each section. Ideally, each PT should be evaluated every two months. The PT should keep a record of scores and review them periodically.

Reflection 6.3

I was fortunate to work for an employer who encouraged personal develop-ment. I had regular unknown evaluations. This stimulated in me a desire to be the best trainer I could be. If your gym does not provide this facility, provide it yourself. Or, if your PT manager is willing, implement your own form of evaluation for your team.

Activity 6.2

Draw up your own self-evaluation sheet. Reflect on the thinking you put into (a) designing the component sequence and (b) describing the 'best practice' that you are aiming at. What does this process teach you?

Guidelines

The following table provides a checklist for each training session. It is particularly useful for a PT's first few workouts, before decisions over session order become second nature.

Each session

1. Client to complete payment agreement form if this is the first session.

2. Meet your client at reception.

3. Consult tracker sheet for the client's goals and/or any protocols.

4. Fill in the date of the session.

5. Ask how they are feeling today (physiologically and/or psychologically).

6. Observe how they look and fill in record sheet.

7. Ask if the client would like to concentrate on any aspect of their goals today.

8. Fill in the aim of this session on the record sheet – very important.

9. Fill in consecutive workout number.

10. Warm up client.

11. Assisted stretch.

12. Main session, including recording of the workout and recording of perceptual responses using shorthand.

13. Cool-down.

14. Assisted stretch.

15. Ask how the client found this session and update the tracker accordingly.

General guidelines for every session

Be professional:

Be aware of progression and continuity.

Tailor the session relative to the client's functional capacity.

Adhere to the tracker specifics.

Attend to the client's needs, e.g. a towel or a water break.

Monitor manual heart rate during the warm-up, main session and cool-down. Use RPE chart for client feedback.

Be aware of your exercise selection and order.

Spot correctly and safely.

Innovate where possible.

Replace any equipment used.

Summary

This chapter has provided the guidance for professional planning and recording of workouts. The tracker provided may be used to keep clients' details to hand and help complete individual records of each workout with the PT. The resulting records build into a library of previous sessions, providing information for a review of the training programme and for session-by-session training decisions. The programme of sessions should develop cyclically and take into account any changes in a client's status. All trainers should use a self-evaluation system. Professional practice of this type is paramount to a PT's success.

Further study

Few texts deal with detailed personal training session planning. One text that does is ACSM (2007) *ACSM's resources for the personal trainer*. This book discusses in more depth some of the areas covered by this chapter.

Useful websites include the following:

- **www.personaltraining1st.com** – blank trackers and record forms are available to download from here;
- **www.exerciseregister.org/** – the Register of Exercise Professionals for the United Kingdom;
- **www.fitnessstandards.org/Practitioners/ethics.html** – an alternative code of ethics for personal trainers to follow.

Appendix: Tracker and record forms

Figure 6.2: Tracker explained

PERSONAL TRAINER
CLIENT TRACKER

WWW.PERSONALTRAINING1ST.COM

CLIENT NAME			TRAINER		DATE			NEXT TEST DATE	
			Trainer 1					*[See note 1.]*	

Special considerations *[see note 2.]*	Pregnancy ☐		Hypertensive ☐		Functional			Other metabolic	
					Knee	Shoulder	Back	IDDM	NIDDM
					☐	☐	☐	☐	☐

Goals	Client's goals			Trainer's quantifiable goals	
	1.			1. *[see note 3.]*	
	2.			2.	
	3.			3.	

Coronary artery disease risk factors	Obesity ☐	Smokes ☐	Age ☐	Diabetes ☐
	Sedentary ☐	High LDL ☐	Hypertension ☐	Family history ☐
	Total risk factors	Is this client a GP referral?	YES ☐	NO ☐
	Intensity recommendations *[see note 4.]*	Low ☐ <60%	Moderate ☐ <75%	High ☐ <90%

Client workout guide	1. *[See note 5.]*
	2.
	3.

Client training notes	1. *[See note 6.]*
	2.
	3.

Testing results	Age	DOB	RBP	BW (kgs)	THRZ	BF%	VO$_2$ max	BMI	WHR

Medical notes	Functional: Coronary: *[see note 7.]* Others:						

CV intensity notes (10 mins)	Bike	Row	TM	Step	X Trainer	VC
	[See note 8.]					

Resistance notes (10RM)	CP	LP	LPD	SP	SPCP	SPSQ	LE	LC	SQ	
	[note 8.]									

Personal information and notes, e.g. sports/interest	1.

Notes

1. Next fitness test.
2. Vitally important that you are aware of special considerations.
3. Trainer's goals should be worked out using measurable variables. For example, the client may refer to aerobic fitness – you can use VO_2 max.
4. Percentage of maximum heart rate that is recommended for this client.
5. The normal structure of the workouts.
6. Client likes/dislikes can go here.
7. GP medical notes.
8. Notes on the intensity setting on CV equipment and on the weight that the client is capable of lifting.

Key

BF%	body fat %
BMI	body mass index
BW	body weight
DOB	date of birth
IDDM	insulin-dependent diabetes mellitus
LDL	low-density lipoprotein
NIDDM	non-insulin dependent diabetes mellitus
RBP	resting blood pressure
THRZ	target heart rate zone
VO_2 max	aerobic fitness
WHR	waist to hip ratio

Figure 6.3: Example of completed tracker

PERSONAL TRAINER
CLIENT TRACKER

WWW.PERSONALTRAINING1ST.COM

CLIENT NAME	TRAINER	DATE	NEXT TEST DATE
Client 1	Trainer 1	02/03/08	12/05/08

Special considerations	Pregnancy ☐	Hypertensive ☒	Functional			Other Metabolic	
			Knee ☐	Shoulder ☐	Back ☐	IDDM ☐	NIDDM ☐

Goals	Client's goals	Trainer's quantifiable goals
	1. *Get fitter* 2. *Lose weight* 3. *Destress*	1. *Increase VO$_2$ max to 40 ml/kg/min* 2. *Decrease BF% to 26%* 3. *Decrease RBP to 135/80*

Coronary artery disease risk factors	Obesity ☒		Smokes ☐		Age ☐		Diabetes ☐	
	Sedentary ☐		High LDL ☐		Hypertension ☒		Family history ☐	
	Total risk factors 2		Is this client a GP referral?		*YES* ☐		*NO* ☒	
	Intensity recommendations		Low ☐ ‹60%		Moderate ☒ ‹75%		High ☐ ‹90%	

Client workout guide	1. *Circuit type workouts* 2. *Increase LBM through resistance training* 3.

Client training notes	1. *Client enjoys circuits that work all muscle groups in one session* 2. *No split routines* 3. *No isometric exercises*

Testing results	Age	DOB	RBP	BW (kgs)	THRZ	BF%	Vo2max	BMI	WHR
	35	14/3/73	142/86	74	120-139	33%	37	31	0.90

Medical notes	*Functional: Knee operation – arthroscopy two years ago; no problems* *Coronary: Slight systolic hypertension – exercise intervention only* *Others:*

CV intensity notes (10 mins)	Bike	Row	TM	Step	X Trainer	VC
	L4	2.80/500m	7 kph	L3	L3	–

Resistance notes (10RM)	CP	LP	LPD	SP	SPCP	SPSQ	LE	LC	SQ	
	30 kg	40 kg	25 kg	15 kg	–	40 kg	20 kg	15 kg	38 kg	

Personal information and notes, e.g. sports/interests	1. *This female client has a young daughter called Evie. She wants to be more active with her and has decided to hire a PT to help.* 2. *She also watches tennis and is a fan of Serena Williams.*

Figure 6.4: Blank record form

Client name: _____ THRZ: _____ BW: _____		WWW.PERSONALTRAINING1ST.COM
Date of session:	Date of session:	Date of session:
Client report:	Client report:	Client report:
Trainer report:	Trainer report:	Trainer report:
Aim of session:	Aim of session:	Aim of session:
Session no.	Session no.	Session no.
Session notes:	Session notes:	Session notes:
Trainer sig: *Mark Ansell*	Trainer sig: *Mark Ansell*	Trainer sig:

Figure 6.5: Example record form

Client name: Client 1 THRZ: 120–139 bpm BW 74 kg		
Date of session: 3/4/08	Date of session: 5/4/08	Date of session:
Client report: *Feels a little tired, but OK*	Client report: *Feels good*	Client report:
Trainer report: *Looks OK*	Trainer report: *Looks rested*	Trainer report:
Aim of session: *Circuit-based muscular endurance RBP taken at 138/84*	Aim of session: *Increase LBM through use of resistance training RBP taken at 134/84*	Aim of session:
Session no. 7 W/U [warm-up] X-trainer 8' ♥122 Str Hams/Quads BWSQ x15 Mod PUPS x15 BW lunge x15 each ⑩ on 1st circuit SROW 15x15x1 DBCR 15x15x1 STEP UPS x15 STAR JUMPS x15 ♥133 on 2nd circuit ♥136 on 3rd circuit ABS x15 BEXT x15 Repeat all above circuit x3 C/D [cool-down] Bike 5' ♥118 at 4' Str Traps/quads/hams RBP taken at 130/82	Session no. 8 W/U Row 2.80/500m 8' ♥124 Str Quads/calves LP 40x10x3 BBDL 30x10x3 ⑩ FCR 20x10x3 FCP 30x10x3 DBOAR 12x10x3 DBSP 7.5x10x3 ⑨ ABS • x30 SMANS x30 C/D Bike 5' ♥116 at 4' Str Chest/quads/hams/lats RBP taken at 132/84	Session no.
Session notes: *Client enjoyed workout*	Session notes: *Should increase DBSP to 9kg next w/o*	Session notes:
Trainer sig: *Mark Ansell*	Trainer sig: *Mark Ansell*	Trainer sig:

WWW.PERSONALTRAINING1ST.COM

Exercise library

One of the main issues I have identified during my personal training career is the need for a mental exercise library. A professional PT should be able to train a client's muscle groups with an array of equipment. He or she will need to be flexible and creative when training in either a gym or a home environment. PTs need to have in their heads a number of different exercises for each muscle group.

The sheer number of exercises combined with equipment options makes for almost infinite possibilities. Example exercises for the chest include machine chest press, barbell/dumb-bell chest press, resistance band press, dumb-bell flyes, pec deck machine, cable flyes, smith press chest press, cable cross-over, press-ups and manual resistance chest press. Many different body part exercises may be combined with methods of execution and variables such as incline (an upward slant), decline (a downward slant), flat (horizontal), isometric, isokinetic, isotonic, plyometric and eccentric. It is the PT's job to convert the various possibilities into actual training sessions.

This chapter is designed to help you:

1. be aware of the possibilities when choosing exercises;
2. develop personal training depth charts;
3. build creativity into your sessions;
4. be aware of when and how spotting is conducted.

Depth charts

The term 'depth chart' has been borrowed from professional sport. In team sports, the coach or manager may use depth charts showing all the combinations in which their players can be used. This means that if, for example, a certain player is injured, the coach knows what options exist for replacements. The 'deeper' the chart, the more possibilities the coach has for covering each position.

PTs can work on the same principle with exercises by generating a list to show the range of the possible exercises for each muscle group. This chapter provides below some sample lists as starting points. The more familiar the PT is with each chart, the more this way of thinking becomes second nature and the PT will be able to switch between exercises without hesitation.

It is important to recognise that such depth charts are more than *just* lists, because they put exercises into rank order (just as a team coach will have a first, second and third choice, say, for each position in the team). For example, if you were training a client's quadriceps muscle group, your depth chart may be as follows:

1. Barbell squat (closed chain, i.e. in contact with the ground, compound muscle, free movement).
2. Smith press squat (closed chain, compound muscle, fixed movement).
3. Dumb-bell squat (closed chain, compound muscle, free movement).
4. Leg press (closed chain, compound muscle, fixed movement).
5. Leg extension (open chain, i.e. not in contact with the ground, isolating muscle, fixed movement).
6. Medicine ball squat (closed chain, compound muscle, light resistance).
7. Body weight squat (closed chain, compound muscle, very light resistance).
8. Wall squats (closed chain, isometric contraction).
9. Manual resistance leg press (closed chain, compound muscle, resistance dependent on PT).
10. Manual resistance leg extension (open chain, isolating muscle, resistance dependent on PT).

The most desirable exercises for the client will be placed at the top of the list. If, however, numbers 1, 2 and 3 are unavailable because, say, the equipment is already in use, then the PT can move on to the next item on the list instead. The order of items on the list will depend on the client's training goals.

Activity 7.1

Try to add five more exercises to the above list to start your quadriceps depth chart.

Reflection 7.1

One of the best trainers I have watched had the ability to train their clients in an almost effortless manner. The trainer could walk into an extremely busy gym and conduct whatever session was necessary, even if most equipment was being used. All of his sessions could be put under scrutiny afterwards and could be shown to have been aimed at clients' specific goals. This was achieved by having a detailed knowledge of his gym environment and by having excellent depth charts for each muscle group.

Muscle groups

The *major* muscle groups that are covered in this chapter are legs, chest, back, shoulders, arms and abdominals/lower back. Beyond these major groups PTs talk in *minor* muscle groups: quads, hamstrings, glutes, hip flexors, adductors, abductors, gastrocnemius, soleus, tibialis anterior (legs), pecs, serratus anterior (chest), latissimus dorsi, rhomboids (back), deltoids, traps, rotator cuff (shoulders), biceps, triceps, forearm flexors/extensors (arms), abdominals, erector spinae, obliques (abs and lower back). Beyond this are the actual proper names and functions for each one of these minor groups. You should be well versed in these muscle names, as you will need to consider exercise effects, for example, whether a dumb-bell raise relates to anterior, medial or posterior deltoids.

Equipment

There are three main categories of equipment available:

1. Free weights – barbells, dumb-bells, kettle bells, body bars.
2. Machines – each working muscle groups slightly differently.
3. Others – resistance bands, dyna bands, medicine balls, sandbags, manual resistance, gym balls, weighted vests, steps and ropes are just some examples.

This chapter could not hope to include every exercise available. We focus on free weight exercises here because machines are mostly straightforward and in any case vary with different manufacturers. As you explore this list, it will become apparent that you will need to research further and build beyond what is shown here. The Internet provides an array of exercises for free or a small fee. A good place to start is **www.exrx.net** – this website has a muscle directory with video demonstrations for many exercises. **www.ptonthenet.com** also provides an excellent resource in this regard. The exercises that you learn and select will help to define your personal *style* as a PT.

One can utilise different methods of execution within exercises. An example is press-ups, where the methods are numerous – including incline, decline, unilateral (one arm), negative, close grip, wide grip, jumping, walking, clapping, one leg up, on knees, box, fist, weighted . . . the list goes on!

A word of warning: when researching new exercises to use, always consider the safety of using them with your clients. You should try them first on yourself or colleagues to assess how viable they are. The exercises may look good, but actual execution may be contraindicated in the case of some clients. ('Contraindicated' here refers to an exercise, the execution of which is inadvisable to a particular client due to high risk of injury or illness.)

Exercise depth charts

Items italicised in the lists below are shown pictorially (Figures 7.1–7.58).

Do remember that the lists below are not comprehensive lists showing all possible exercises: they are to be used as a starting point for your own depth charts.

Legs depth chart
Barbell squat
Barbell lunge
Barbell step-up
Barbell calf raise
Barbell dead lift
Romanian dead lift
Machine: leg curl, leg extension, leg press, adduction, abduction, seated calf raise, cable tibialis anterior

Chest depth chart
Barbell chest press
Dumb-bell chest press
Dumb-bell chest flyes
Press-ups
Machine: chest press, pec deck, cable cross-over

Back depth chart
Barbell bent-over row
Dumb-bell one-arm row
Cable seated row
Dumb-bell pull over
Dumb-bell reverse flyes
Machine: seated row, lat pull down, reverse flyes, chin-ups

Shoulder depth chart
Barbell shoulder press
Dumb-bell shoulder press
Barbell upright row
Dumb-bell lateral raise
Dumb-bell shrugs
Cable lateral raise
Dumb-bell arnies
Machine: shoulder press, cable internal/external rotation

Arms depth chart
Barbell bicep curl
Dumb-bell tricep extension
Cable bicep curl
Dumb-bell hammer curl
Dips
Reverse curls
French press
Preacher curls
Dumb-bell bicep curls
Dumb-bell tricep extension
Forearm barbell/dumb-bell wrist extension/flexion
Machine: bicep curl, tricep extension

Power depth chart
Barbell power clean
Barbell push press
Snatch
Power pull

Abdominal/lower back depth chart
Crunch
Back extensions
Superman
Plank
Extended leg crunch
Knee rolls
Bridges
Cat backs
Mackenzies
Bicycles

Manual resistance depth chart
*Chest press**
*One-arm row**
*Leg extension**
*Leg curl**
*Bicep curl**
*Tricep extension**

* Illustrated in Chapter 9.

Legs depth chart exercise examples

Barbell squat

Start position (A) – knees slightly wider than shoulder width apart and not locked, bar evenly rested on the shoulders.

End position (B) – straight back, knees at no more than 90 degrees, head up, knees not over toes.

Figure 7.1: Barbell squat (A)   Figure 7.2: Barbell squat (B)

Barbell lunge

Start position (A) – knees slightly wider than shoulder width, barbell evenly distributed on the shoulder.

End position (B) – both knees to 90 degrees, head up, back straight, creating a lunge.

Barbell step-up

Start position (A) – feet slightly wider than shoulder width, head up, bar evenly distributed on shoulders.

Middle position (B) – step up with right leg with foot fully on step.

End position (not illustrated) – bring up left leg on to the step, pause, then reverse the process, stepping down with the left leg first, then right leg to start position.

Figure 7.3: Barbell lunge (A)

Figure 7.4: Barbell lunge (B)

Figure 7.5: Barbell step-up (A)

Figure 7.6: Barbell step-up (B)

Barbell calf raise

Start position (A) – barbell rested on shoulders evenly weighted, balls of feet rested on step, knees straight but not locked, head up.

End position (B) – raise the heels of the feet together, keeping all other body parts stationary, head up, isolate the gastrocnemius muscle.

 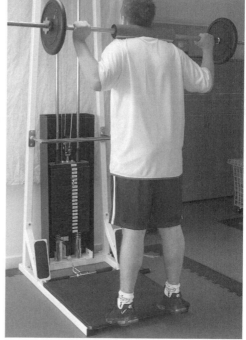

Figure 7.7: Barbell calf raise (A)   Figure 7.8: Barbell calf raise (B)

Barbell dead lift

Start position (A) – feet shoulder width apart, keeping the back absolutely straight, pick the bar up off the floor, keep the head up.

End position (B) – extend the hips and knees, keep back straight at all times, keep the bar close to the body, stand up straight.

Chest depth chart

Barbell chest press

(Using eccentric contraction, normally starting from a weight rack.)

Start position (A) – five-point contact: head, shoulders, lower back, two feet; grip slightly wider than chest, bar held above the chest.

End position (B) – extend arms, don't lock elbows, bar staying above the chest line.

Figure 7.9: Barbell dead lift (A)   Figure 7.10: Barbell dead lift (B)

Figure 7.11: Barbell chest press (A)   Figure 7.12: Barbell chest press (B)

Dumb-bell chest press

Start position (A) – five-point contact: head, shoulders, lower back, two feet; hold dumb-bells just above chest.

End position (B) – extend the arms so that the dumb-bells are above the chest and arms are straight but not locked.

Figure 7.13: Dumb-bell chest press (A)

Figure 7.14: Dumb-bell chest press (B)

Dumb-bell chest flyes

Start position (A) – five-point contact, head, shoulders, lower back, two feet; arms slightly bent out to the side, controlling the dumb-bells.

End position (B) – keeping the arms in the same position, move the dumb-bells up over the chest meeting at the mid-point.

Figure 7.15: Dumb-bell chest flyes (A)

Figure 7.16: Dumb-bell chest flyes (B)

Back depth chart

Barbell bent-over row

Start position (A) – arms straight, even grip, back straight, legs slightly bent.

End position (B) – be very careful that the lower back does not move, flex the elbows and bring the bar to the chest, head up at all times.

Figure 7.17: Barbell bent-over row (A)   Figure 7.18: Barbell bent-over row (B)

Dumb-bell one-arm row

Start position (A) – one knee rested on the bench, other leg slightly bent, back straight, arms slightly bent.

End position (B) – keeping all other body parts still, flex the elbow and lift the dumb-bell up to the chest making sure that the elbow stays tucked in near the body.

Figure 7.19: Dumb-bell one-arm row (A)   Figure 7.20: Dumb-bell one-arm row (B)

Cable seated row

Start position (A) – feet placed on the foot rests, legs straight but not locked, back and arms straight.

End position (B) – keeping the upper body totally still, pull the V bar towards the sternum, making sure that the arms are kept by the sides.

Figure 7.21: Cable seated row (A)

Figure 7.22: Cable seated row (B)

Dumb-bell pull over

Start position (A) – five-point position, head, shoulders, lower back, two feet; hold the dumb-bell above the head with slightly bent arms.

End position (B) – pull the dumb-bell up and over the head keeping the arms in the same position.

Figure 7.23: Dumb-bell pull over (A)

Figure 7.24: Dumb-bell pull over (B)

Shoulder depth chart

Barbell shoulder press

Start position (A) – feet shoulder width apart, grip wider than shoulders, knees slightly bent.

End position (B) – push the bar upwards, keeping the body in one position, don't lock the elbows.

Figure 7.25: Barbell shoulder press (A)

Figure 7.26: Barbell shoulder press (B)

Dumb-bell shoulder press

Start position (A) – back rested against the seat, dumb-bells held at shoulder height, feet on the floor.

End position (B) – push the dumb-bells upwards until the arms are nearly straight but not locked.

Figure 7.27: Dumb-bell shoulder press (A)   Figure 7.28: Dumb-bell shoulder press (B)

Barbell upright row

Start position (A) – feet at shoulder width, knees not locked, arms in close grip.

End position (B) – keeping elbows high, pull bar up to just below the chin, making sure all other body parts are kept still.

Figure 7.29: Barbell upright row (A)   Figure 7.30: Barbell upright row (B)

Dumb-bell lateral raise

Start position (A) – knees slightly bent, feet shoulder width apart, back straight, dumb-bells held by the sides, arms slightly bent.

End position (B) – raise the dumb-bells up to be level with the shoulders, making sure that all other body parts are completely still.

Figure 7.31: Dumb-bell lateral raise (A)

Figure 7.32: Dumb-bell lateral raise (B)

Dumb-bell shrugs

Start position (A) – knees slightly bent, back straight, hold the dumb-bells by the sides.

End position (B) – raising the shoulders only, bring the dumb-bells up to hip height, keeping the rest of the body completely still.

Cable lateral raise

Start position (A) – feet shoulder width apart, knees slightly bent, cable held across the body.

End position (B) – pull the cable across the body up to shoulder height, keeping the rest of the body still.

Figure 7.33: Dumb-bell shrugs (A)   Figure 7.34: Dumb-bell shrugs (B)

Figure 7.35: Cable lateral raise (A)   Figure 7.36: Cable lateral raise (B)

Arms depth chart

Barbell bicep curl

Start position (A) – knees slightly bent, EZ bar held with elbows close to the body.

End position (B) – keeping the body position still (especially the lower back), raise the bar up to the chest, make sure that the elbows are locked into the sides of the body.

Figure 7.37: Barbell bicep curl (A)   Figure 7.38: Barbell bicep curl (B)

Dumb-bell tricep extension

Start position (A) – knees slightly bent, back straight, support one arm with the hand of the other. Bend the arm with the dumb-bell over the shoulder keeping all other body parts still.

End position (B) – extend the arm and, only bending at the elbow, bring the weight up over the head. Remember that there should be no movement apart from the elbow.

Cable bicep curl

Start position (A) – feet shoulder width apart, arms by the sides, knees slightly bent.

End position (B) – keeping all body parts completely still (especially the lower back) raise the bar to the chest using the full range of movement in the biceps.

Figure 7.39: Dumb-bell
tricep extension (A)

Figure 7.40: Dumb-bell
tricep extension (B)

Figure 7.41: Cable bicep
curl (A)

Figure 7.42: Cable bicep
curl (B)

Power exercises depth chart

Barbell power clean

Position (A) – back straight, hands wider than shoulder width, head up, feet shoulder width apart.

Position (B) – draw the bar upwards keeping the head up, back straight, bar near the shin area, completed at speed.

Position (C) – scoop the bar upward keeping it near the body, extend the knees and hips. Start to use the momentum created by the legs into the bar. Do not attempt a reverse the curl at this point.

Position (D) – bring the bar sharply up and catch it near the shoulders using the momentum created by the legs. Flex the knees at the catch.

Position (E) – extend the knees and hips, bringing the bar to rest at shoulder height.

Figure 7.43: Barbell power clean (A)

Figure 7.44: Barbell power clean (B)

Figure 7.45: Barbell power clean (C)

Figure 7.46: Barbell power clean (D)

Figure 7.47: Barbell power clean (E)

Push press

Start position (A) – feet shoulder width apart, back straight, grip shoulder width apart, bend the knees into a quarter squat position.

End position (B) – using the momentum provided by the legs, push forcefully upwards until the bar is in a shoulder press position. Do not lock the knees.

Figure 7.48: Push press (A)

Figure 7.49: Push press (B)

Abdominal/lower back depth chart

Crunch

Start position (A) – lie on back with knees bent. Feet flat on the floor, hold the abdominal muscles.

Middle position (B) – raise torso, slide hands up thighs, raise shoulders off the floor.

End position (not illustrated) – return to the starting position.

Figure 7.50: Crunch (A)

Figure 7.51: Crunch (B)

Back extension

Start position (A) – lie on front with hands on lower back.

Middle position (B) – raise torso up, keeping neck relaxed.

End position (not illustrated) – return to the starting position.

Figure 7.52: Back extension (A)

Figure 7.53: Back extension (B)

Supermans

Start position (A) – lie on front with hands and legs extended. Raise right arm and left leg, then return to the floor.

End position (B) – repeat with the left arm and right leg.

Figure 7.54: Supermans (A)

Figure 7.55: Supermans (B)

Plank

Lie on front, come up onto the elbows keeping the back absolutely straight. Maintain this position statically by contracting abdominals and lower back muscles. Hold this position for 30 seconds to one minute.

Figure 7.56: Plank

Extended leg crunch

Start position (A) – lie on back, raise the legs up and then contract the abdominal muscles. (Extra resistance can be provided using a medicine ball or powerbag.)

Middle position (B) – raise the shoulders off the floor keeping the arms straight, pushing the hands towards the feet.

End position (not illustrated) – lower slowly back to the start position.

Figure 7.57: Extended leg crunch (A)

Figure 7.58: Extended leg crunch (B)

Spotting

Spotting is when you assist your client in the safe lifting of a weight. As well as providing greater safety, the spotter can help to motivate the client by providing verbal encouragement during each set. Spotting also provides the PT with the perfect opportunity to check the technique of each lift and to provide the client with feedback as needed. One often overlooked benefit to spotting is the kinaesthetic feedback available to the trainer, who can feel the client lifting the weight through a bar or the client's limbs. This allows the PT to provide assistance only when it is required. The PT can learn through practice how much help to provide for each lift attempt. Obviously it is important to allow the client to lift as much as they can rather than provide the *trainer* with the workout!

One aspect for new personal trainers to consider is the personal space factor when spotting their clients. The PT must overcome the 'fear' of getting near to the client – the PT needs to be in the right place to provide assistance. This involves getting 'in there' with the client and invariably means physical contact.

It is also important to make sure that the PT is in a safe body position in order to remain focused when spotting. That means not responding to external stimulus until the lift is complete. For example, if one's mobile phone rings, it clearly needs to be ignored. It is also possible to spot machine exercises, so long as the PT is fully aware that weight stacks can trap fingers if care is not taken.

Communication is vital when spotting. The client requires clear commands when taking and receiving weights. 'My bar' is a common phrase that can be used to indicate that either of you has the weight under control. It should also be made clear how many reps are to be attempted in a spotted set; this allows both parties to understand when fatigue is likely to occur.

Below are some spotting techniques for selected exercises:

- Dumb-bell chest press and flyes – hold the wrists of the client, not the elbows, as the client can fail and drop the dumb-bell into their face.
- Barbell chest press – make sure that your lower back is in the correct position to take the weight if needed. Two hands under the bar, alternate grip (this is where one hand is in an open grip, palm up and the other is closed, palm down).
- Shoulder press – you are behind the client and then hand the weights to the client with their hands at shoulder height. Again, the client's wrists should be held for safety.
- Barbell upright row – you are in front of the client, your hands in an alternate grip on the barbell.
- Barbell squat – contrary to popular belief, you can spot squats by being positioned behind the client with your hands on the client's lower rib area. As the client performs the squat you should follow the movement pattern to provide assistance if needed. Step-ups and lunges are spotted in a similar manner. You must remember to move with your client in all three of these exercises. If a power rack is being used by the client, it is better to use two spotters. One spotter should be positioned each side of the barbell with their hands cupped under the ends of the bar, following the movement of the barbell and providing assistance simultaneously if needed.

- Dumb-bell lateral raises – you are behind the client and your hands should follow the movement of the client's elbows.

Warning

You must be aware of your own safety, the client's and that of other gym users when spotting. If at any point the client fails on standing exercises and the weight is descending, remember to get out of the way! Also remember that power exercises are *never* spotted. That includes cleans, push press and power pulls, the reason being that they include a momentum phase where it is too dangerous for a spotter to be in close proximity.

> ### Reflection 7.2
>
> *I find it amazing that even placing my hands below a barbell on a chest press can make the client think that I am providing assistance when in fact I am not. Most clients will believe that they can lift more with extra help, even when I'm not actually providing it!*

Pulse raisers

Other exercises that you can utilise within your sessions are called pulse raisers. These are good for warming up and circuit-based workouts. Here is a range of examples, some unilateral (using one limb at a time, e.g. when running) some bilateral (using limbs simultaneously, e.g. feet-together jumping):

- skipping (using a rope);
- star jumps (jumping with legs spread to the sides and bringing the arms up simultaneously to shoulder height);
- compass jumps (feet move bilaterally to all points of the compass);
- boxing (includes variations of punches);
- bunny jumps (good for ski training);
- astrides (on a bench, bilaterally jumping onto and off);
- ski jumps (unilateral wide-leg hops);
- slalom jumps (bunny jumps that mimic ski movement);
- burpee (squat thrust followed by star jump);
- sprint starts (squat thrust position, but unilateral leg movement);
- shuttle runs (between two cones);
- spotty dogs (splitting the feet alternately as in a lunge and bringing the same arm up to level with the shoulder during the movement);
- dumb-bell punch (using light dumb-bells to 'punch out' with);
- running arms (as in running, just forget the legs);
- high knees (bring the knees up in front to level with the hips).

These exercises are useful with home training clients, as little equipment is required.

Active learning

With a training partner, try any exercise that you haven't experienced. Then, once you have mastered each movement, try spotting each exercise for your partner. When you see or research a new exercise, attempt it in a safe environment and, if you think that it can be used, add it to your mental library. It may help to keep a pocket book that contains details of your known exercises. Add to this as your personal training career develops.

Summary

You should now start to realise the potential number of exercises that are available for each muscle group and therefore the possibilities when choosing exercises. This will lead you nicely into the development of your own depth charts, which are an essential part of your PT persona. The creativity aspect comes to the fore when you start to add to your depth charts with new variations of exercises and innovative ways of using equipment.

This chapter has also given you some clear guidelines on how to use spotting techniques. You need to develop these techniques alongside your depth charts to make sure that your exercises are performed in a safe manner by your clients.

A good start for your depth charts is when you have approximately 20 exercises per muscle group. With this you should be able to train your client in almost any gym environment. The real test comes when you have little or no equipment as in home training. When you can conduct a 45-minute session using only a towel and a 3x2 metre mat space, you have developed your exercise knowledge and built your depth charts.

Further study

Example exercises are available from a variety of texts and, as mentioned above, the Internet is a good place to start building your exercise library.

www.exrx.net – an excellent starting point.
www.ptonthenet.com – this site contains a large exercise library, although this is a subscription service.
www.brianmac.co.uk – some descriptions of dumb-bell exercises.

One text that covers 300 exercise examples is *The Gold's Gym training encyclopaedia*:

Grymkowski, P, Connors, E, Kimber, T and Reynolds, B (1984) *The Gold's Gym training encyclopaedia*. McGraw-Hill.

The weight training and body building press is another good resource. These magazines carry example exercises every month for different muscle groups.

Chapter 8

Fitness testing

'Fitness testing' is a general term for physical testing both of athletes and the general population. Fitness testing can be used to help determine health status as well as providing base-line levels of fitness. From the 1950s, coaches and athletes have recognised that data from tests could be applied to the design of training programmes and subsequent goal setting. The development of sport and exercise science has refined fitness and sport professionals' understanding and use of data.

Personal trainers have been offering fitness tests for many years, both within fitness facilities and at clients' homes. Testing is now an accepted skill for a PT to possess. If a PT knows a client's fitness status, this will enhance the client's training experience and sense of PT professionalism.

This chapter has been designed to help you:

1. understand the relative benefits of field versus laboratory based fitness testing;
2. recognise the importance of health screening;
3. individualise the choice of testing;
4. be able to administer a series of tests;
5. know how to use testing to enhance motivation with a view to your client achieving their goals.

Principles of fitness testing

All fitness testing must be scientific in nature. The PT should strive to make testing as accurate and scientific as possible. This requires correct and safe administration of tests related to the client's individual needs. Data from tests will need to be compared to gender and age-related tables. This process is termed 'interpretation of data' and is required in order to 'grade' the client. This will indicate the degree of fitness and identify which elements of fitness need to be improved.

Rationale of fitness testing

All fitness trainers, personal trainers, sport scientists and coaches use fitness testing in one form or another. It is so ingrained in physical training that you need to be aware of at least the minimum requirements for health screening clients. For most clients, testing should be used at regular intervals – for example, monthly for body fat percentage and bi-annually for aerobic fitness tests.

Common purposes include:

- essential health screens;
- client needs analysis;
- goal setting;
- programme effectiveness;
- sport-specific testing.

Fitness testing is an important tool in the personal trainer's repertoire. This chapter will provide you with some initial protocols. It is recommended that you also use the research resources mentioned in order to increase the battery of tests that you can use.

Ideally, testing should first be done at the start of a client's training, to help the PT to ascertain the needs of that client. During the programme, or during periodised cycles, clients should be retested in order to measure the effectiveness of training. If the client has sport-specific goals, it is useful to research and apply tests that are specific to their sport. This may even involve liaising with a sports coach to maximise the client's progress.

Performing fitness tests well provides an opportunity to demonstrate professionalism. It also allows the PT to discuss the client's goals in the light of the results. The results can be used to educate clients when discussing the physiological adaptations outlined in Chapter 3. In some respects, education of the client is as important as the physical training in sessions as it allows the client to achieve their goals more readily. Test data can be used to motivate the client.

Reflection 8.1

The use of test results has proved valuable in setting goals for many clients I have trained in the past. I would recommend tailoring testing for each individual and setting the goals accordingly, otherwise the process can backfire and demotivate the client! Be careful to take into consideration the client's goals and not to veer off track with irrelevant needs analysis. An example of careful goal setting was when I was training a particular hypertensive client. The lowering of his blood pressure was the primary goal, but he also wanted to train to increase his muscle mass. This posed me with a tricky problem. I had to focus on the primary goal by testing his blood pressure both before and after the workout, while also providing endurance repetitions so as to work towards a secondary goal of improving his aesthetics. The trick was to work within the protocol for hypertensives, but also cater for his secondary goal within sessions.

All tests need to be valid and reliable. To be valid, tests must be rooted in sound and justifiable research. In this context, validity relates to whether the test actually indicates what it does. For example, a bleep test (described later in the chapter) indicates that it tests a client's aerobic fitness. Because it provides a score for VO_2 max (the maximum amount of oxygen a client can utilise in one minute), this can be termed a valid test. Reliability refers to test/retest data. For example, if you had a client perform the bleep test with the correctly administered protocol two days apart with the same regime prior to each test, the result would be the same. Similarly, the result should not vary according to who is administering the test.

It is important for personal trainers to understand the differences between field and laboratory-based testing. Most personal trainers do not have access to such fitness-testing equipment as cycle ergometers or treadmills. Gas analysis is even less likely to be used by trainers. Therefore, the protocols discussed in this chapter will focus on field-based testing with indications as to the contemporary laboratory tests. There will also be an indication of the industry-recognised 'gold standard' test for each aspect of fitness that is being tested.

The five main categories of fitness that can be tested are:

- aerobic (including cardiovascular fitness);
- anaerobic (including strength tests);
- muscular endurance;
- flexibility;
- body composition.

Reflection 8.2

I have used both laboratory and field-based tests for a variety of clients and have found that the results from field-based tests can be valid and reliable. It is, however, always essential to implement protocols properly.

Each client will have specific goals that the trainer should be working towards and a test or tests should be chosen relative to the client. There is no point in testing using a predetermined list of tests; these may not be relevant to the client and could even prove detrimental to their motivation. Use empathy when choosing tests for clients. It may not be entirely appropriate to attempt a fat calliper test on a client who is obviously clinically obese!

Testing sequences

The order of each test should follow this pattern:

- Explanation.
- Demonstration.
- Administration.
- Interpretation.
- Feedback.

If many tests are to be administered in one session, note that the recommended order is as follows:

1. Resting pulse.
2. Resting blood pressure.
3. Any body-composition testing.
4. Strength tests.
5. Anaerobic capacity.
6. Muscular endurance.
7. Aerobic capacity.
8. Flexibility.

The reasons for using this order are found within the test results themselves: you could not hope to gain a resting pulse after an aerobic test. Testing for strength using 1 RM testing is unsafe if it is done after muscular endurance due to muscular fatigue. Flexibility is best tested at the end of the testing regime as the tissues are warmer and the process can form part of a cool-down for the session.

Health screening

Health screening is vital to the consultation session with every client and should be used on a retest basis depending on the client's health status. It cannot be stressed enough that screening must be administered to every client in order to protect the client and the trainer. Screening can provide information on the exercise and injury history of the client and indicate potential risks. For example, hypertensive clients will need pre- and post-blood pressure readings *every* session in order to ensure that they are within acceptable ranges for training. Without this screening, the PT can be liable for 'duty of care' breaches and in extreme cases be sued for damages. All reputable fitness organisations such as the ACSM and NSCA recommend unreservedly the use of health screening for *all* clients.

A PAR-Q (physical activity readiness questionnaire) form should be used as the absolute minimum standard of screening. Examples of PAR-Q forms are readily available to download from the Internet; the Canadian Society for Exercise Physiology produces an excellent PAR-Q and, provided it is not altered, can be photocopied for use at **www.csep.ca/communities/c574/files/hidden/pdfs/par-q.pdf**.

If your client answers 'yes' to any of the questions, this will require a referral to their GP with a letter from the trainer.

Health and lifestyle questionnaires

Questionnaires provide a useful means for finding out background information about clients in a short space of time. They should be used in the initial consultation session. They expand on the PAR-Q and allow the trainer to ask the client a predetermined series of questions about them, to ascertain information from their eating habits to their training status. An example of a health and lifestyle questionnaire can be found at the end of this chapter.

Informed consent

Prior to *all* testing the client should complete an informed consent form which lists and gives the opportunity to 'delete as appropriate' the tests that are being administered in that session. This informed consent form will help to cover the personal trainer as it gives the client an opportunity to disclose any clinical conditions that would affect the safety of the test on that particular day. The personal trainer must keep all forms (PAR-Q, health and lifestyle, and informed consent) on file permanently in case of future legal issues.

Reflection 8.3

I keep all the completed client forms in a locked metal filing cabinet at home. If there is a need to refer back to any form for any client, it is a simple process as they are stored alphabetically by surname. You can also keep records that are colour-coded according to the client's medical status. I have used different coloured folders for high-risk metabolic problems, functional problems and asymptomatic clients in order to see at a glance who is most at risk.

A question you may ask when reading and implementing the following protocols is why should you use these methods over others? The answer is that each protocol described has been used by coaches and personal trainers many times. All tests are tried and tested methods of fitness testing with particular reference to personal trainers.

Protocols

Field-based protocols are particularly relevant to the personal trainer because of their ease of use, the portability of the equipment and the relatively low cost. Field-based tests are outlined here in order to help you administer them to your clients, along with other alternatives.

Blood pressure

This is used as an essential health screen at the start of any consultation, as well as a periodical screen for asymptomatic clients and pre- and post-workout for hypertensive clients. It is widely recognised that manual sphygmomanometers (sphyg) with a stethoscope are superior to automatic models so long as the personal trainer is well versed in the method of usage. An aneroid (dial) sphyg is probably the best bet for a personal trainer to acquire as they are light and will not take up much room in a kit bag. For the protocol regarding taking a manual blood pressure reading, see ACSM (2005).

The two measurements of blood pressure are systolic and diastolic (expressed as a fraction). The systolic pressure is the pressure of blood in the vessels when the heart contracts (i.e. the maximum pressure); diastolic pressure is the pressure of the blood between heartbeats when the heart is at rest (i.e. the minimum pressure). Healthy values in adults are around 120/80.

It is *essential* to remember that if the reading is above 159 systolic and/or 99 diastolic the PT *must* refer the client to their GP for medical clearance before any physical activity programme commences.

Resting pulse

Using the radial artery (wrist) palpate the pulse and count the beats for 30 seconds, then double for a beats per minute figure.

Body composition

Body mass index (BMI)

BMI is the most basic tool in trying to ascertain a client's body composition. The equation takes into account a client's height and weight. The result can then be related to normative data.

BMI is calculated by the following equation:

$$BMI = weight\ (kg) / height\ (m)^2$$

Consider the following example:

- Client's weight = 70 kg.
- Height = 1.74 m.
- $1.74^2 = 3.03$
- 70/3.03 = 23
- A BMI of 23 is in the normal, healthy range.

BMI normative data:

- <20 – underweight;
- 20–25 – healthy weight;
- 26–30 – overweight;
- >30 – obese.

You must be aware that BMI has limitations; the calculation does not take into account muscle mass, so a bodybuilder would score very high, even though they would be extremely lean.

Activity 8.1

Work out and interpret BMI scores using the following data:

- *Client 1: weight = 91 kg, height = 1.76 m.*
- *Client 2: weight = 104 kg, height = 1.36 m.*
- *Client 3: weight = 66 kg, height = 1.55 m.*

Waist to hip ratio (WHR)

Another important health test is to ascertain where body fat is stored. Using girth measurements we can compare a client's waist circumference against their hip circumference. WHR is calculated using waist circumference (cm) / hip circumference (cm). Use a tape measure to gain your data (both readings are taken with the client standing). At the narrowest point between the umbilical point (belly button) and bottom tip of the sternum, measure the waist circumference. The hip circumference is the widest point around the hips with the client standing with their legs together and their buttocks relaxed.

Data suggests that a figure exceeding 0.95 for males and 0.86 for females would be a significant health risk due to the storage of fat near their major organs. For example, your male client has a waist circumference of 123 cm and a hip circumference of 115 cm; 123/115 = WHR ratio of 1.07. This indicates that your client is at high risk of disease.

Girth measurements

Girth measurements can be used in goal setting for your clients. Those who wish to increase their muscle mass would be ideal subjects in girth measurement assessment. Goals could be based on realistic size increases across their bodies.

Other girth site measurements you can use with your clients are bicep, thigh, calves, chest and forearm. These are particularly useful with clients who want to build muscle; you can measure these sites once a month to check progression.

Skinfold callipers

This is the preferred method of body composition analysis. The error of estimate is less than bio electrical impedance (see later in this section for details) and it is fairly cheap to buy the plastic variety of callipers. There are various methods using a different number of skinfold sites to calculate body fat percentage. Here the 'four site sum' method will be outlined (ACSM, 2005).

You need a set of callipers, a tape measure and a pen. The callipers can be around £20 for the plastic type or £180 for the superior Harpenden type.

1. Mark on the right side of the body the location of each of the four skinfolds: the suprailiac, tricep, thigh and abdomen.
2. Pinch the skin diagonally at the suprailiac site so that 1 cm of fat is visible, then put the calliper on and allow the tension to release for no more than two seconds. Read the value in mm. *Do not* pull the callipers off – it hurts!
3. The tricep is taken vertically in the same manner.
4. The thigh is slightly more tricky and is a vertical fold.
5. The abdomen reading is taken vertically.
6. Once all measurements are taken, you should retake them twice in sequence. This provides a total of three readings for each site. This allows the subcutaneous fat (i.e. the fat deposited beneath the skin) time to reform, whereas if you take three readings at the same site in immediate succession, the fat just under the skin that you are measuring will not have re-formed back to a normal state and may provide an incorrect reading.

7. All readings should be within 2 mm of the others for that site. An average reading of the three should be used.
8. Once you have average readings for all four sites, add them together ('sum 4') and put the result into one of the following equations.

For women:

0.29669 (sum 4) – 0.00043 (sum 4 squared) + 0.02963 (age) + 1.4072 = percentage body fat

For men:

0.29669 (sum 4) – 0.005 (sum 4 squared) + 0.15845 (age) – 5.76377 = percentage body fat

Consider the following example:

The client is a 34-year-old man and the sum of the four skinfolds is 85 mm.

85 mm 0.29669 (85) = 25.22
0.005 (7225) = 3.61 [7225 is 85 squared]
0.15845 (34) = 5.39
(25.22 – 3.61) + (5.39 – 5.76377) = 21.23623

which, when rounded to the nearest figure, gives us a body fat of 21 per cent.

Site definitions:

- *Suprailiac* – get your client to find the top of their iliac crest (the bony prominence at the top of the pelvis) – this saves you prodding about their abdominal area! The mark should be immediately above the iliac crest with a diagonal line.
- *Tricep* – exactly halfway between the elbow and shoulder joints in the midline of the belly of the tricep – a vertical fold.
- *Thigh* – on the front of the thigh midway between the line of the groin and the top of the kneecap (patella) – a vertical fold.
- *Abdomen* –a vertical fold 2 cm just to the side of the umbilicus (belly button).

Activity 8.2

Insert the following results into the above equation:

- 22-year-old male with sum of skinfolds of 102 mm.
- 45-year-old female with sum of skinfolds of 91 mm.
- 19-year-old female with sum of skinfolds of 98 mm.

Other methods of working out skinfold body composition involve more or fewer body sites, tables and other equations. If you find the skinfolds described here to be problematic, try other site methods. It is highly recommended that you practise on as many volunteers as possible to become proficient, as administrator variability can be a factor in inaccurate measurement.

Reflection 8.4

Skinfold callipers are an absolute must. I carry the plastic callipers in my kit bag as they are light and accurate enough for body fat measurement at any time. With any test, the time it takes you to gain reliable data will decrease as you get used to the methods of testing.

Bio electrical impedance and hydrostatic weighing

Bio electrical impedance (BEI) is an alternative method to estimate body fat, which can be fairly inexpensive if you use the handheld or scales method of testing. The machine will pass a small electrical current around your client's body, measuring the difference between body tissues that obstruct (impede) the current and those tissues that conduct the current, then calculating body fat from this reading. The problem with these machines is that a specific protocol must be followed by the client before testing. Not all machines are very accurate.

Hydrostatic weighing is the gold standard of body composition testing. It involves weighing the client in and out of a water tank – something that is highly unlikely to be used by a personal trainer!

Strength tests

Hand grip dynamometer

Dynamometers can give you a method of ascertaining your client's strength with one piece of portable equipment. This piece of equipment is not essential, nor necessarily the cheapest or best way of gaining strength data. If you have access to a hand grip dynamometer, the protocol is straightforward: get the client to adjust the hand grip to the size of their hand and then ask them to grip as tightly as possible while lowering their arm to the side of their body. This will give a reading of the strength of the hand and forearm muscles – there is a link between this reading and overall body strength.

1 RMs

An alternative method is to use repetition maximums ('1 RMs'). This is a superior method of determining your client's strength (the amount that a client can lift once, i.e. one repetition), usually using barbells in maximum bench press and squat exercises to gauge all-over body strength.

Anaerobic capacity

Stair run test

This test can be easily administered on any staircase and although there is scant normative data, it does supply a measure of the client's anaerobic capacity. Using this test periodically will monitor the effect of power training over time. You must measure the height of the stairs in metres (the number of steps multiplied by the height of one step) and weigh the client in kilograms. The client should run as fast as possible up the stairs (stepping on each step) while you record the time in seconds. Use the following equation to calculate the energy used:

Energy = distance x force (using weight x 10: the constant used for gravity) = 'X' joules

Here: distance = height of the stairs in metres and
weight = client weight in kilograms

Power (measured in watts) = energy/time.

The energy in joules is divided by the time it takes for the client to run up the stairs to give the total power output. This figure can be improved over time and so can be used in goal setting. The fact that weight is taken into account can be linked with body composition figures, and power outputs will increase with an increase in muscle mass.

Activity 8.3

Example: step height is 2.3 m, the client weighs 70 kg and the time taken is 2.5 seconds.

Energy = 2.3 x (70 x 10) = 1610
Power = 1610 / 2.5 seconds = 644

The client uses 644 watts of power in running up the stairs.
Now calculate the power used in the following examples:

- Client 1 weighs 54 kg, step height is 2 m and the time taken is 2.5 seconds.

Activity 8.3 continued

- Client 2 weighs 79 kg, step height is 2.9 m and the time taken is 4.1 seconds.
- Client 3 weighs 92 kg, step height is 3.4 m and the time taken is 5.5 seconds.

Wingate cycle ergometer

This anaerobic test requires a cycle ergometer – usually a Monark bike will be used in a laboratory setting. The test is a 30-second maximal effort cycle by the client in order to estimate their maximum power output and ultimately to indicate their anaerobic capacity. The client's body weight determines the resistance on the cycle's flywheel and they are instructed to put 100 per cent effort in from the start of the test. The results are given in watts. This is the recommended test when working with athletes who have a need for anaerobic testing.

Muscular endurance

Press-ups and curl-ups

These two tests provide the easiest administration protocols within personal training. The press-up test involves getting the client into the full press-up position for males and the modified (knee) press-up position for females, then getting them to perform the full press-up exercise until exhaustion occurs. The numbers of full, completed press-ups are then compared to normative data (see, for example. **www.brianmac.co.uk/pressuptst.htm**) to indicate how good their upper body muscular endurance is.

The curl-up test involves the client lying on their back in a curl position with their arms out straight, knees bent and palms down on their thighs. The client must perform repetitions where the hands reach the top of the knee on the up phase and the head does not quite touch the floor on the down phase. Again, the number of completed repetitions may be compared to normative tables to indicate muscular endurance of the abdominals (see **www.brianmac.co.uk/curluptst.htm**).

Alternative muscle group muscular endurance tests are given below.

Chin-ups

Chin-ups require the use of a chin bar. You can utilise the home variety of chin bars which fit into door frames for this purpose, though a gym-based chin station would be preferable. The client will perform full chin-ups until fatigue occurs and the number of completed chin-ups compared to normative tables (e.g. **www.brianmac.co.uk/chinstst.htm**).

Free weight tests

Free weight tests can be used, for example, for testing for bicep brachii muscular endurance. Using light dumb-bells, get the client to perform as many repetitions as possible. Usually, these tests will only be used for individual goal-setting purposes as the normative data is less readily available.

Aerobic capacity

Bleep test

The infamous bleep test is a maximal test. It will take a client up to the maximum capacity they can take, i.e. their maximum heart rate. There are, therefore, serious safety considerations, especially relating to heart problems. Only use this test with asymptomatic clients, to be on the safe side.

The test estimates VO_2 max, that is, the maximum amount of oxygen that an individual can utilise in one minute. This is the best figure for ascertaining a client's aerobic capacity as it relates directly to oxygen usage. It is expressed in millilitres.

You will need two cones, a CD player, a CD with the test protocol, a 20 m tape measure and the interpretation tables. Measure 20 m in a straight line and put a cone at either end of the 20 m, explain to the client that they must jog up to the cones to the sound of a bleep. If they miss more than 2 cones in a row, the test is terminated. You must also explain that there are health risks to this test and they are in control during the test. The test will gradually increase in rate and repetitions in ascending levels until the client can no longer maintain that pace. You must record the level and shuttle when the client became fatigued and look up their VO_2 max score from tables that are usually supplied with the CD.

The bleep test has a good validity and reliability rating. The main concern for you may be finding a safe 20 m area – local parks are ideal for this test.

Reflection 8.6

When I have used the bleep test I have found that the motivation of the client is the single most important factor in gaining a good VO_2 max reading. You must make sure that your client has the will and determination to complete the test to exhaustion.

Tecumseh step test

This test uses recovery heart rate to gauge how fit your client is and is not as accurate as VO_2 max tests. You can use a client's staircase or a box for this test. Step tests are generally the method used by personal trainers as they need little space and equipment. You will need a step of 20.3 cm (8 in) in height, a stopwatch and a metronome (this produces a beat at a constant pace). Explain to the client that this test is submaximal and will require them to step in time to the metronome at 96 beats per minute, i.e. in right foot up, left foot up, right foot down, left foot down cycles for three minutes continuously. A demonstration by you will generally help the client understand what is required. After they have stepped for the three minutes, get them to sit down while you find their radial pulse; 30 seconds after they have completed the test, take their pulse for another 30 seconds. This figure should then be put into a gender and age-related table to find out the aerobic fitness of that client.

VO₂ max cycle ergometer tests

Various protocols are available for testing clients on bikes – those from YMCA, ACSM and WHO are just a few. They are accurate when using submaximal protocols and extremely accurate when using maximal heart rate protocols. If gas analyses of oxygen, carbon dioxide and air volumes are monitored, they become a definitive indication of your client's aerobic fitness. The problem for the personal trainer is one of laboratory equipment usage. However, if you get the chance to perform or study any of the laboratory tests mentioned in this chapter, it is recommended that you do so.

Treadmill tests

Again, the personal trainer will only have access to treadmill tests within a gym or testing laboratory. They are usually a very good method of testing aerobic fitness. All VO_2 max tests should try to replicate the main mode of activity of the client. The treadmill should be used for runners, the cycle ergometer for cyclists. Tests for rowers usually take place on a Concept2 rower (see **www.concept2.co.uk/**).

Flexibility

Goniometer

Flexibility testing is important for some clients, mainly those who have limited range of movement at certain joints. A classic example is that of office workers having tight hamstrings due to sitting for long periods of time. A goniometer is an inexpensive and light piece of equipment that can be kept in your kitbag to measure joint angles. You need to align two arms of the goniometer to meet the two bones around the joint to be measured. The protractor part should be set at zero at the point of full extension and the client should move their body part to their full range. You can then take the reading.

Activity 8.4

The hamstring should be measured with one end of the goniometer aligned with the spine and the other with the femur; the protractor should be over the hip joint. The client will be lying on their back for this and you may have to assist the leg up to a point when the client will tell you that they feel a strong stretch. At this point read the value on the protractor. A potential safe range for the hamstring would be around 60–120 degrees.

Safe ranges of flexibility for the hamstring are shown in Figure 8.1. If a client has restricted range of movement or hyperflexibility (excessive flexibility), this may lead to an increased risk of injury.

Sit and reach box

A sit and reach box is an alternative method used in gyms to estimate the lower back and hamstring flexibility. The client sits on the floor facing the box with their legs straight and their feet touching the box, then stretches forward with one hand on top of the other to reach as far as they can along a scale in centimetres on the top (horizontal surface) of the box.

Figure 8.1: Potential safe and increased risk ranges for hamstring flexibility

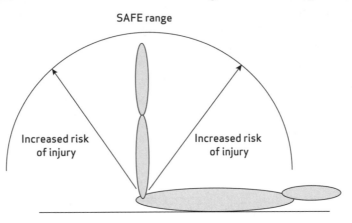

Reflection 8.7

The least flexible client I have trained came out at around 35 degrees for a hamstring reading. This obviously needed careful session planning as the man's hamstring muscle group was extremely tight. There was significant flexibility training incorporated into his workouts as a direct consequence of the results from this test.

Fitness testing kit

A summary of the ideal kit to build up to for fitness testing (in order of necessity):

- Manual aneroid sphyg and stethoscope.
- Stopwatch.
- Calculator.
- Small tape measure.
- Plastic callipers.
- Metronome.
- Goniometer.
- Handgrip dynamometer.

Subsequent purchases can upgrade your equipment. For example, a set of Harpenden callipers will last a lifetime if they are looked after properly.

Practical activities and exercises

Administer all the recommended tests, in the order given, on asymptomatic friends or colleagues. Record your experiences throughout each test. This will allow you to achieve two things: you will get more proficient at those tests and it will point you in the direction of researching further tests if you do not gel with a particular testing protocol. For example, you may prefer other skinfold sites to the ones listed here.

Activity 8.5

Consider which fitness tests may be appropriate and which inappropriate for the following clients:

- Bill is 63 years old and needs a hip transplant.
- Jim is 19 and wants to focus on fitness for soccer.
- Marie is 27 years old, clinically obese and gets out of breath quickly.
- Hannah is 20 years old and seems nervous when in the fitness facility.
- Tasha is 30 and wants to lose body fat and get fitter.
- Graham is 39 years old and does not seem to understand technical jargon.
- Alesha is 23 years old and indicates that she is not interested in any testing.
- Marcus is 33 years old and wants to know exactly how generally fit he is.

The American College of Sports Medicine (ACSM) produces invaluable guidelines when administering fitness tests. **www.acsm.org** is a highly recommended website to visit.

Summary

You should now be aware of the importance of health screening before administering any physical test on your clients. It cannot be stressed enough that this aspect of fitness testing is mandatory in order to protect you and the client. Once you have decided that it is safe to proceed, you need to consider which tests are appropriate for that client – testing for health, fitness or sport must be individualised. When you have acquired the data and interpreted the values, they can be used to motivate your clients. It is still important to remember that not all clients will respond well to constant goal setting and numerical data. The PT must use common sense! Overall, fitness testing offers the personal trainer and fitness coach an excellent tool to enhance the client's training experience and motivation.

Further study

NSCA (2000) *Essentials of strength and conditioning* 2nd edition. Human Kinetics.
YMCA (2000) YMCA fitness testing and assessment manual. 4th edition. Human Kinetics.

The following websites give protocols to various tests and further reading ideas:

www.topendsports.com/testing/
www.exrx.net/Testing.html

Figure 8.2: Health and life style questionnaire

Health and lifestyle questionnaire				
Instructor name:				
Date:				
Personal details				
Name:				
Date of birth:				
Age:				
Sex:				
Tel:				
Mobile:				
Occupation:				
Emergency contact:				
Height:	Weight:			
Medical history				
Please tick if you have experienced any of the following medical conditions:				
	Tick	Date		
Pregnancy				
Lung problem				
Heart problems (e.g. angina)				
Arthritis				
Stroke				
Allergy				
Diabetes				
Asthma				
High blood pressure				
Epilepsy				
Cancer				
Osteoporosis				
High cholesterol				
Other (please specify)				
Is there an immediate family member who has a history of heart disease before the age of 55 years?				
Please circle:	Yes	No		
Do you have any functional problems (e.g. shoulder, knee or hip problems)?				
Please specify:				
Are you taking any medication?				
Your exercise history				
Do you currently exercise?	Yes	No		
If so, how many days per week on average?				
If you used to perform exercise why did you stop?				
Do you currently smoke?	Yes	No		
Do you drink alcohol?	Yes	No		
If so, how many units per week approximately?				
Exercise expectations				
Is there any specific goals for your exercise programme (e.g. weight loss, muscle mass or toning)?				
Usage				
How many times a week will you be using the gym?				
Personal preferences				
Is there any type of training or piece of equipment that you want/do not want to use?				

Chapter 9

Advanced training techniques

There are many advanced training techniques (ATT) that can be used by the personal trainer, some originating from sports training, others from health-related fitness. The sport techniques can be utilised both in-house and externally to offer new and varied workouts. The health-related techniques may be mandatory when working with client groups drawn from special populations. This chapter will outline some examples of both types of advanced techniques.

The more training techniques PTs are familiar with, the more varied the type of clients they can work with. If a team sport player comes to a PT for training, then speed agility quickness (SAQ) training will provide a starting point. If working with a hypertensive client, on the other hand, the PT needs to follow the specific training guidelines for such clients in order to ensure that their health is not put at risk.

This chapter is designed to help you to:

1. use SAQ training in PT sessions;
2. understand the science and implementation of plyometric training;
3. know how to use manual resistance training in PT effectively;
4. recognise that there is an array of equipment that can be used in ATT;
5. gain an introductory understanding of periodisation;
6. apply knowledge of special population training when dealing with health clients.

Speed agility quickness

SAQ training dates back to the ancient world. The Romans understood the need for specific agility training for their fighters in the gladiatorial arena. Although athletes today do not have to worry about dodging weapons of war, the same principles have been honed and developed during the twentieth and into the twenty-first century. If an athlete can combine speed with direction changes and quickness of feet, this will provide a competitive edge. Even for non-athletes, SAQ can provide welcome variety in training and help clients to work towards non-sport goals such as aerobic fitness.

Starting SAQ training

The client receiving SAQ training needs to understand the need for 'quick feet'. This can be achieved by getting the client to walk on their toes, then their heels, and then the balls of their feet. It should become apparent that the most stable and 'ready' walk is provided by the balls of the feet. This is where the client should focus during SAQ training.

SAQ drills need to be implemented in ascending order of difficulty, thereby allowing the client to learn the 'feel' of SAQ training. The following tables provide a starting point for an SAQ training exercise library.

1. Single plane (forwards and backwards) movement, on the balls of the feet throughout.

Level 1	Level 2	Level 3	Level 4	Level 5	Level 6
Walking on the balls of the feet	Skipping, moving forwards	Feet to backside	High knee walk	Elbow punch with trainer	High walking skip
Keep toes up and heels off the floor.	Make sure of minimal floor contact.	Pull heel to buttock.	Bring the knee to the chest and bounce.	The client stands in front of the trainer.	There should be minimal floor contact.
This improves ankle stability.	Small skips only.	Use speed in this drill.	Keeping the hip flexors working throughout.	The trainer holds their hands out and the client pumps the arms to 'punch' the trainer's hands.	Arms should be used in a pumping action.

2. Multi-plane movement (if training for sport, this should mimic the movement pattern).

Level 1	Level 2	Level 3	Level 4
Side-step skip-overs	Lateral skips	Side-step skip running	Backwards skip
Utilising the learnt skipping movement.	Keep high knees throughout.	These include step-overs.	Should be performed with wide legs.
Make sure that the client builds speed into this drill.	Build speed into these.	Make sure the leading foot crosses in front of the body.	This prepares the client for back pedalling.

3. Ladder drills – using a ladder specially made for this type of training that rolls up for easy transport. It is laid horizontally on the ground and has either plastic or nylon rungs. All drills should build in speed once the drill is learnt.

Level 1	Level 2	Level 3	Level 4	Level 5	Level 6	Level 7
Quick feet	Straight run	Two-foot run	Lateral runs	Run in, run out	Moving star jumps	Run in, run out frontal
On balls of feet, learning how to miss the rungs.	Place one foot on the ground between each rung.	Make sure that both feet touch the ground between each rung.	Both feet to touch the ground between each rung, side-on running.	Facing the side of the ladder, move laterally while putting both feet in each rung and out again.	Perform one star jump in between each rung while moving forwards.	As two-foot run, but with added complication of stepping outside the ladder, on alternate sides.

4. Mini hurdle drills – these hurdles range from 10 to 50 cm in height depending on the functional capacity of your client.

Level 1	Level 2	Level 3	Level 4	Level 5	Level 6
One-foot walk	Straight run	Two-footed walk	Two-footed run	Random lateral changes	Hurdle compass jumps
These can be bilateral (both feet walk over the hurdle) or unilateral (one foot to the side of the hurdle).	One foot contacts between hurdles.	Both feet have to contact between hurdles.	Both feet contact, done at speed, build a sprint in at the end of the hurdles.	The client performs lateral running while you shout a verbal cue for them to change direction.	Place four hurdles in a square, the client jumps over one hurdle and returns to the middle. Each hurdle is jumped in succession.

The work to rest ratios should follow general energy system training guidelines. If the client is working at a higher intensity, they will need more rest between sets. Repetitions will depend on the energy system being trained or sport-specific timings.

Activity 9.1

1. Try the drills above yourself. This will give you an idea of how they feel when a client attempts them. After you have attempted them, find a volunteer to try the training points on. This will allow you to gain confidence when using these drills with your clients.
2. Write an SAQ programme for a client named John who has hired you to train him for his amateur rugby team. Use a sample of all levels of drills and a mixture of the exercises.

Interest can be added to SAQ programming by using different scenarios for clients to visualise. A good example is provided by the historical example above: the client can be programmed as a gladiator for a session. This is not too difficult as the exercises above can be modified for the purpose. Another scenario would be American football, where SAQ is used widely in almost all positions within the sport. An American football can be provided as a specific cue for the client at the start of such a session.

Extension SAQ information

SAQ sessions can utilise sports movements and timings. Football players, for example, can perform SAQ work from a rolling start. One can recreate lane training, where the client can start with a slow acceleration and then sprint just before a change in direction signalled by a verbal cue.

To increase speed alone, various methods of sprint training may be used. Overspeed sprint work can be implemented using a decline of 3–10 per cent to allow the client to improve stride frequency, one of the components of speed. Alternatively, resistance may be used to slow the client down. This can be achieved by using resistance cords held by the PT. If there is a sled available, this can be loaded with weight (usually no more than 10 per cent of the client's body weight) for the client to drag. This resistance will improve the length of the client's stride and the strength of the running movement pattern.

Read and react drills are another method for improving clients' reaction and agility. Reaction balls may be used. These may be thrown by the PT; when they land, they bounce at random and the client must chase them. It is essential to ensure that there is plenty of space during this exercise. Alternatively, the PT can provide the sport-specific movements needed for read and react drills; the client has to move whenever the PT moves.

Plyometrics

Plyometrics uses pre-stretching of the muscles to create an increase in the resultant force production during the execution of the exercise being performed. The term plyometrics was not used until the mid 1970s when it really began to take off in Western countries. Some people use the term 'jump training' for plyometrics. It was in Eastern Europe that bounding and jumping were first utilised to great effect in athletics. If you have an opportunity to watch film of East European athletes using plyometrics during the late 1960s to early 1970s, I would strongly recommend it. Some of the training sequences are amazing and were well ahead of their time.

The outcome of plyometrics is primarily concerned with an increase in power output. Therefore, the nature of plyometric training is intense, with varying degree of difficulty in the exercises. Only conditioned clients should train in this way. There are different criteria for deciding which clients meet this requirement. One of the simplest methods is to see whether the client can perform a 1 RM squat at 75 per cent body weight, a 5 RM squat with 60 per cent of body weight in under five seconds, and at least five clapping press-ups. If so, they might well be ready to start a plyometric programme. Consideration must be given to floor type: the flooring must absorb some of the force produced by the client. Grass, a mat or carpet will suffice; concrete will not! The client's footwear must also be inspected for suitability. The training shoes must have some 'bounce' as provided by cross-training shoes. The client should not use squash trainers for this type of training.

Physiological aspects

Plyometric training allows clients to use the stretch reflex, initiated by the muscle spindle when the muscle is stretched, to increase the force production of the muscle. The increased force production is directly related to the degree of stretch experienced by the muscle – the more stretch, the more intense the reflex. One of the properties of muscle tissue is elasticity (the ability of the muscle to return to its original length after being stretched). Plyometric training manipulates the muscle's elastic property.

There are three phases to all plyometric exercises:

1. The landing (or eccentric contraction).
2. Amortisation.
3. The take-off (or concentric contraction).

The idea is that, when the client lands, the muscle stretches and the muscle spindle instigates the stretch reflex. The amortisation phase is the time spent on contact with the floor and is crucial: too long and the client will lose the stretch reflex. The take-off uses the elastic energy stored in the landing phase, thereby increasing the force of the muscular contraction. This is otherwise known as the stretch shortening cycle.

The following exercises provide a platform from which to launch plyometric programmes. Equipment can be used for some of these exercises – for instance, cones, boxes (or platforms), hurdles and medicine balls. It is important before beginning to ensure that the client knows how to land properly – with bent knees that are just over the toes and leaning forwards with a straight spine after landing.

Category	Jumps in place	Standing jumps	Multiple jumps	Platform jumps	Upper body	Bounding
Level 1	Hopping between cones	Standing long jump	Hexagon drill	Single-leg jumps	Jumping press-ups	High-leg skips
	Simple hops (not over cones).	Also a fitness test.	You need to mark out a hexagon (rubber markers are good for this).	One foot on the ground, one on the box, then jump.	A small distance off the floor between reps.	Bounding skips with arms out in front and full hip flexion evident.
Level 2	Dynamic lunges	Take-off drills	Lateral cone jumps	Lateral box jumps	Rebounding medicine ball drills	Dynamic walking lunges
	Jumping lunges, can be switching legs in mid air.	Three bouncing steps and a jump.	Usually three cones that the client will jump over and back again.	To the side of the box, then jump on the box and off, repeat.	These will need a wall or angled trampet.	Lunges with a bound.
Level 3	Standing pike jump	Standing long jump and lateral runs	Stair two-foot hops (hands on head)	Multiple box jumps	Clapping press-ups	Single-leg bounding
	The classic pike position on the spot – this is hard!	Can be in any direction as needed.	Make sure not to use concrete steps.	Using two or more boxes in a line, jump up and down.	Full claps in between – too easy? Do them behind your back!	Can lead with one leg throughout or changing legs.

The use of medicine balls is particularly useful in upper-body and platform drills. Upper-body medicine ball work includes chest passes, seated twists, overhead throws and caber tossing. Medicine balls can add resistance in platform drills, though holding the ball makes the client less able to balance. A weighted barbell can also be used to good effect in plyometrics. The jump squat and dynamic lunges are lots of fun with the added weight of a barbell! The resistance in jumping can be provided by jump mats that have resistance bands attached to the client and the mat. As the client gains height, the resistance increases, providing a great workout.

Manual resistance

One measure of a PT is the ability to train almost any client with almost any goal with a minimum of equipment. The following guide will help with this. Manual resistance (MR) is where the personal trainer provides the resistance for the client to work against. In effect, the PT takes the place of free weights, machines and fitness equipment. The minimum equipment needed is a gym towel. MR is ideal for home-training clients and provides gym-based clients with variety in their workouts. MR was first used in the ancient world, much like SAQ. The armed forces have more recently used MR due to the lack of equipment available in the field. With creativity they have found that most exercises can be performed with a partner – for this reason MR is sometimes called partner-assisted resistance.

The advantages of MR are that:

- it needs little equipment;
- it is inexpensive;
- it can be performed anywhere;
- eccentric contractions by the client can be felt by the trainer (there is no cheating!);
- the trainer can control the speed and level of resistance;
- it can provide variety in your workouts;
- it allows the trainer to track range of movement and exercise technique.

The disadvantages are that:

- the resistance lifted cannot be measured;
- if the client is capable of heavy lifting, the PT needs to be able to provide sufficient resistance.

Some trainers have questioned the effectiveness of MR when fatiguing their clients; this attitude usually lasts only until they try it for themselves! The resistance that even smaller trainers can exert is usually more than enough to tire clients, especially in isolating exercises. Part of the reason for this is that there is no cheating within reps. When training with weights the client can release the weight on the controlling, or eccentric phase. This is not possible in MR as the trainer can feel both the concentric and eccentric phases. As the client gets into position to perform each exercise, the PT must make it clear that the muscle contraction made by the client must include both the creating (concentric) and the controlling (eccentric). (The easiest way to achieve this is to get the client either to push or pull – depending on the exercise – against you in the controlling phase.) Anyone who has been through a full MR workout will tell you that this element of eccentric force provides ample resistance.

General programming guidelines should still be followed when using MR. The resistance goals should not be changed. For example, for hypertrophy goals the client should still be working at 8–12 reps to fatigue for 3–5 sets. The difference is that the PT gets a workout too!

MR exercises include:

- Upper body: chest press; seated row; one-arm row; chest flyes; bicep curls; tricep extension; press-ups; dips; shoulder press; lateral raises; front raises; upright row.
- Lower body: leg press; leg curl; leg extension; calf raise; adduction; abduction; tibialis anterior.
- Abs: crunch; back extension; plank.

Some MR exercise illustrations

Chest press
Link palms with your client's and track the chest press movement while providing the resistance.

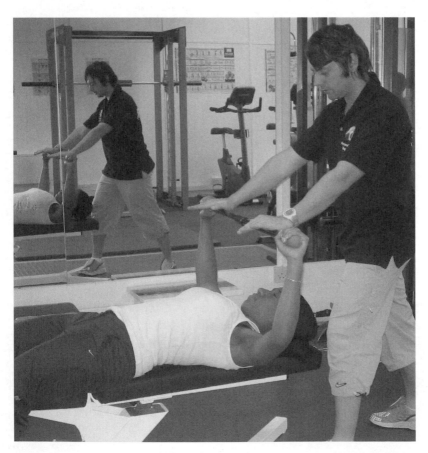

Figure 9.1: Manual-resistance chest press

One-arm row

Make sure that the client's arm tracks near to their body.

Figure 9.2:
Manual-
resistance
one-arm row

Shoulder press

You may need to get your client to sit on the floor in order to provide enough resistance.

Figure 9.3:
Manual-resistance
shoulder press

Bicep curl

This can be unilateral or bilateral as needed.

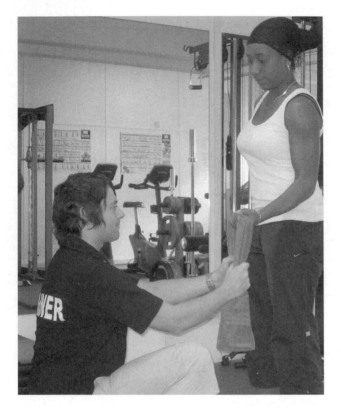

Figure 9.4:
Manual-resistance
bicep curl

Lateral raise

This can be unilateral or bilateral as needed.

Figure 9.5:
Manual-resistance
lateral raise

Leg curl

This is surprisingly effective in fatiguing the hamstring muscle group.

Figure 9.6:
Manual-
resistance
leg curl

Leg extension

You need to put one of your arms under the client's leg to stabilise the knee joint.

Figure 9.7:
Manual-
resistance leg
extension

Leg press

If the PT finds it difficult to provide the necessary resistance when using this exercise with stronger clients (due to the major muscle groups being used), then pre-fatigue the legs using the two lower body exercises above.

Figure 9.8:
Manual-resistance
leg press

Bar bent-over row

This shows the advantage of using a bar that breaks down to fit in your kitbag. The bar allows the client to perform extra exercises that are difficult to perform with a towel.

Figure 9.9:
Manual-resistance
bar bent-over row

Bar tricep extension

Make sure that the client does not move the shoulder joint during this bar exercise.

Figure 9.10:
Manual-resistance
bar tricep extension

Activity 9.2

Now that you have some sample exercises, you need to go out and try them on your clients or a willing volunteer. When you have exhausted the list above, try other exercises that traditionally use weights for resistance. You will be surprised how many exercises can be performed using manual resistance.

Next, write three sessions where you are only allowing yourself to use MR and pulse raisers and you have no equipment to hand apart from a towel. Make one session circuit based, one aimed at a hypertrophy client, and the last for a muscular endurance lower body and abs workout. When you have finished them, go over your notes and MR exercise depth charts to see how you can improve them.

Reflection 9.1

I use manual resistance predominantly with home clients where I have found it extremely effective. Sometimes I incorporate MR into gym sessions as it provides a change from traditional equipment and some clients respond well to this type of training. A word of warning, though: make sure that your client is OK with the increased amount of physical contact between you both. I have had a couple of clients who have not said directly that they found MR intrusive, but I have 'read' the signs and discontinued MR when I felt it necessary.

Equipment and future trends

As mentioned, you can use medicine balls, cones, mats, towels, hurdles and platforms in your ATT sessions. There are other pieces of equipment available too. They include:

1. Weighted vest – this is worn by the client to provide added resistance during any weight-bearing activity and is especially useful when performing plyometrics. The vest is vastly superior to ankle and wrist weights as these place added strain on those joints.
2. Boxing gloves and mitts – boxing workouts provide excellent cardiovascular and muscular endurance workouts. Practise punches such as straights, hooks, crosses, uppercuts and body with a partner. Remember that as a PT you will be exclusively on the mitts providing a target for the client to hit, so practise this predominantly.
3. Weighted bags – the twenty-first century version of boulders and sand bags. Get your clients to hold these or use them as weights to complete traditional exercises.
4. Kettle bells – a Russian export that has been used for physical training for many years. Some trainers use these in many of their sessions. They are meant to be used in multi-plane, multi-joint activity and therefore are deemed 'functional'. With any functional training, be sure that you are working towards your client's primary goal at all times. Kettle bells may not be suitable for all clients.
5. Swiss, or gymnastic balls – not only used in ATT, but generally too. There is some more advanced training that can be performed using a Swiss ball. Leg curls are fun, along with impact bouncing and using the ball for press-ups. All Swiss ball training should be carefully monitored to ensure that the client is capable of advanced work as they can be dangerous in the wrong hands.

Reflection 9.2

I visit a trade exhibition at least once a year to inform myself about the industry and to have a go with new kit. One piece of kit that I have recently used is a system that uses two discs that look like Frisbees. These discs are stood on by the client and can be used in CV or body weight exercises. They are relatively cheap, light for your kitbag and can provide something different for your clients to try. Although this is one new piece of kit that I have integrated into my sessions, I give all new kit a thorough try for myself to make sure that it is appropriate and safe before I let my clients loose on it.

Periodisation

Periodisation is literally a training programme that uses periods of different activities. There are changes in intensity, volume and modes of training depending on the sport or goal of your client. In Chapter 2 we outlined the general adaptation syndrome proposed by Selye. Periodisation puts this idea into practice, using supercompensation to achieve optimum adaptation within the client's physiology. (Supercompensation is a period of reaction by the human body to training overload above resting levels.)

So why do personal trainers use periodised programmes?

1. It promotes progression within a programme.
2. It can decrease the likelihood of overtraining syndrome (or overstress).
3. Such programmes allow optimal use of time.
4. The programmes can be sport specific for athlete clients.
5. Periodisation has been used extensively by sports coaches and is a valid method of programming.

The periods in such programmes have 'cycles' of time frames. The smallest is a microcycle, which lasts about one week. A mesocycle is medium term and can last from weeks to months. A macrocycle lasts a year or more. An Olympic athlete will have a four-year periodised programme that will indicate what training they will be doing (even down to the *day*).

How difficult do you think it would be for you to construct this type of programme?

As long as you build the programme carefully from micro through to macrocycles, you will end up with a sound programme. Though programmes vary between sports, the periodised programme will generally have four periods:

1. Preparatory – this period will deal with the athlete's base conditioning training. Hypertrophy, endurance, strength and power will be concentrated here depending on the primary goal.
2. Transition 1 – this is a short 'break' period and will allow the athlete time to concentrate on the upcoming competition.
3. Competition – peaking occurs here, as you want your athlete client to be at their best. Both volume and intensity of training will drop here and the athlete will focus on technique and strategy training aspects.
4. Transition 2 – this is post-competition and will involve active and fun activity to keep the athlete 'ticking over' before they re-enter the programme at period 1.

Period 3, that of competition, will vary considerably between sports. Think about a Premiership footballer and, in contrast, a 110 m hurdler in track athletics. Consider the differences in the number of competitions and the duration of a competitive season. In fact, the four periods above can be termed pre-season, season, post-season and off-season. This should highlight the importance of periodising athlete (and some of your health clients') programmes.

Periodised programmes may be represented graphically (see Figure 9.11).

Periodised programmes can also be represented graphically to highlight changes in intensity, volume and technique training. An example can be found in Figure 9.12.

As you can see, intensity, volume and technique training all have different values at different time periods within the periodised programme. The PT needs to decide where these three elements should peak, depending solely on the goals of the client.

A yearly periodised programme

Period	Preparatory period			Competition period		Transition 2
Sub-period	General conditioning	Specific conditioning	Transition 1	Pre-comp	Main competitive season	Active recovery
Macro cycle						
Micro cycle						

Figure 9.12: Example of volume, intensity and technique changes within a periodised programme

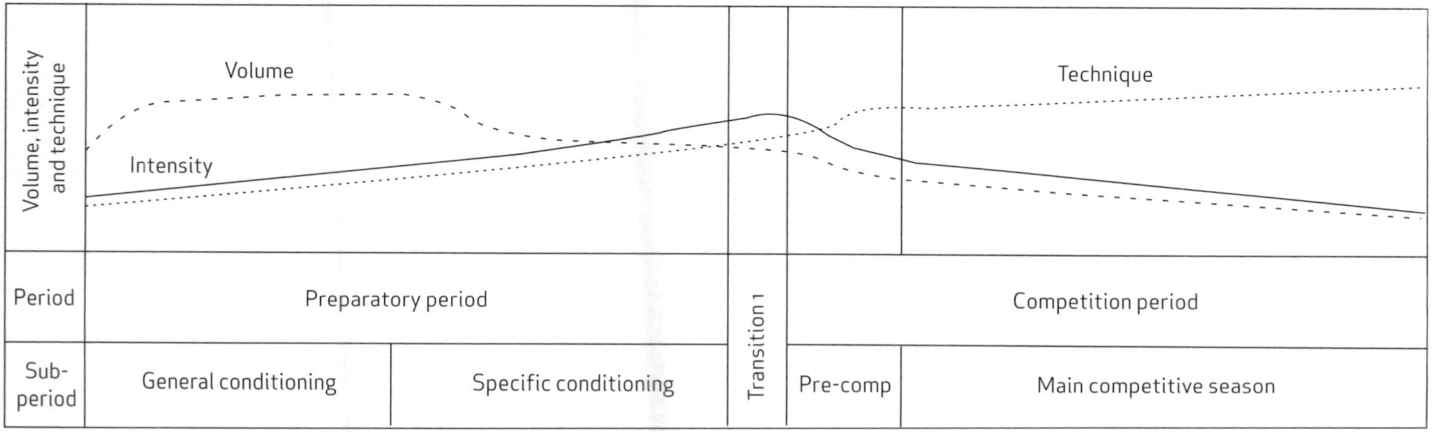
Volume, intensity and technique
Volume
Intensity
Technique
Period
Preparatory period
Transition 1
Competition period
Sub-period
General conditioning
Specific conditioning
Pre-comp
Main competitive season

Periodised programmes for some athlete clients can be very complicated, so it is important to practise writing some smaller programmes before attempting a large-scale yearly version. Periodised programmes can promote exercise adherence and client retention: they enable clients to see the 'big picture'. It is important to remember that all such programmes must be based on client goals, needs analysis and fitness testing.

Activity 9.3

1. Research different periodised programmes for a variety of sports that professional coaches have constructed. You will see that they can vary considerably between sports and even coaches within those sports. Some of these periodised charts are extremely detailed and you should strive to understand each element within them.

2. Using the sample table in this chapter, construct a periodised programme for a client of your choice. It can be any sport, but should include the training regime right down to the individual day. Once completed, construct an intensity, volume and technique diagram that represents where your client should be concentrating their efforts at a particular timeframe. This will give you practice for the construction of real periodised programmes for your clients.

Special populations

Clients who suffer from a diagnosed health problem require special treatment. It is important to apply the information given here and regularly to seek out new and revised guidelines for any clients from special populations. Such careful attention is required by the PT's duty of care.

Hypertension

A client's high blood pressure may be highlighted during the initial health screen. If so, the PT must refer the client to their GP before *any* physical training activity takes place. Professional associations have slightly different definitions of high blood pressure. The threshold which seems the most sensible is 159/99 mmHg. If your client is above in both or either of these readings, the PT must write a referral letter to their GP detailing when and where the reading took place and requesting a letter back that will clear the client for physical activity. Ideally, the GP's letter will also include intensity guidelines. Most hypertensives will have a 70 per cent MHR ceiling placed on their training intensity. This can be increased if their blood pressure lowers naturally over a period of training. It is important to ask hypertensive clients whether they are on any current medication, as this will artificially lower their blood pressure. Where the client is on medication, heart rate cannot be used as an indicator for intensity; RPE must be used instead. Hypertensives must not use the valsalva (breath holding) manoeuvre as this will cause an exponential rise in blood pressure, putting the client at risk.

Cardiovascular exercise is especially applicable for hypertensive clients as the evidence for a positive effect is overwhelming. Due to chronic vasodilation, the resistance to blood flow lowers and blood pressure will drop. Isometric activity must not be performed with this client group as the blood pressure increases seen in this type of training would be dangerously high and could cause a coronary event. Resistance exercises should focus on major muscle groups and promote muscular endurance repetitions. For hypertensives the ACSM recommends a frequency of 3–7 days for 30–60 minutes and an aim of 700–2000 total kcal weekly expenditure.

It is essential to take a hypertensive client's blood pressure both pre- and post-workout to make sure that the client is capable of training. If the reading is more than 200/115 mmHg in either systolic or diastolic, the client should not be trained.

Pregnancy

It has long been known that exercising while pregnant tends to be beneficial for both mother and baby. Mothers have reported better weight control, improved recovery from the labour and less back pain.

The main concern for the PT is their combined safety. There are guidelines available for the PT to follow. If the mother is not a current exerciser when she first approaches the PT, she should first be referred to her GP. After GP clearance, low-intensity workouts should be provided. The PT needs to have a clear idea of what each trimester during the pregnancy will entail. The most obvious consideration is that the baby is constantly growing! This means that the PT does not need to get the client to lift a lot of weight: body weight exercises wherever possible as the woman will be gaining weight anyway.

During the first trimester (the first three months) most of the programme that the woman would normally be following can be used (as long as it is not plyometrics!). There should be *no* stretching *at all* administered to a pregnant client, as a hormone called relaxin is released into the body to facilitate the stretching of the abdomen. The hormone does not affect only the abdomen; it affects the joints too, so they can go beyond a safe ROM.

Trimester 2 needs more consideration as the woman will not be able to perform prone exercises and will not be able to perform any abdominal work. This does mean, however, that she should do pelvic floor work, continue body weight exercises using higher repetitions (12–20) and use compound exercises. The use of RPE should be used to gauge intensity, as the client's heart rate will be affected by the presence of the baby. The ceiling should be an RPE of 12–13 (on the 6–20 scale recommended in Chapter 2), which is a moderate intensity.

The third trimester will almost certainly involve a shorter time in training as most women will find physical training sessions more difficult towards the due date. You should implement quad position activity with a limited standing lying change during the workout. Swiss ball squats, high incline press-ups and the pelvic floor exercises are some examples of training that should be used at this late stage. More general guidelines include the following:

- The client must keep well hydrated during the session.
- Concentration on client posture should be evident in sessions.
- Listen to the client at all times and ask how she finds a particular activity.
- No fatigue should be evident (in contrast to normal workouts).
- The cool-down should be longer, with 5–15 minutes to be used as a guide.
- Be aware of ambient temperature and do not run the session in periods of high humidity and temperature.

Some examples of contraindications for exercising during pregnancy are:

- pregnancy causing hypertension;
- any history of pre-term labour;
- multiple births (twins or above);
- consistent bleeding during the second and third trimesters.

It is highly recommended that if you have a pregnant client, you research this client group further through the ACSM.

Diabetes

There are two forms of diabetes: non-insulin-dependent diabetes mellitus (NIDDM) and insulin-dependent diabetes mellitus (IDDM). Insulin-dependent diabetics need regular injections of insulin as their bodies do not regulate the production of this hormone correctly. PTs need to be aware of both types.

IDDM clients must be referred to their GP for advice and can then train with the following guidelines:

- The client must be able to easily monitor their blood glucose levels, ideally just before and after exercise.
- Carbohydrate intake may be necessary if blood glucose level is below 100 mg/dl (5.5 mmol/l).
- Ensure that the client is aware of the footwear issues surrounding diabetics. Diabetics exhibit circulation problems, nervous tissue degradation, increased risk of infection and a decrease in the ability to heal blisters. All of these problems will especially affect the feet.
- If blood glucose level is more than 300 mg/dl (16.5 mmol/l), do not train the client at all.

NIDDM clients are similar to the above with the following differences:

- Most of these clients will be NIDDM through being obese and therefore weight and fat loss is usually a primary goal.
- Physical activity enhances the regulation of insulin and glucagon hormones, and therefore can reverse the condition with chronic training – good news!

Obesity

If an obese client is unused to performing physical activity, training sessions must be of low intensity to begin with until an aerobic base is evident. The use of exercise in conjunction with a calorie-controlled diet is paramount in tackling the problem from two directions. General guidelines include the following when working with obese clients:

- They should be exercising 5–7 days per week, for 40–60 minutes per day.
- Intensity should be a maximum of 70 per cent MHR with new clients.
- Low-impact exercises are preferable.
- Overall weekly exercise kcal expenditure should be between 1,000 and 2,000 kcal.
- A mixture of CV and resistance activity is appropriate (circuit type).

Respiratory disease, including asthma

Most respiratory disease clients encountered will be asthmatics. They must have their medication with them at *all* times during a workout. This will normally be in the form of an inhaler. The PT should check every session to ensure that the client has the inhaler to hand. There are no intensity recommendations currently for respiratory disease clients. The PT does, however, need to be aware of exercise-induced asthma (EIA) clients, as they are obviously more prone to an asthma episode during your sessions. Exercise overall has been shown to improve lung function and have a positive effect on this client group. CV activity is particularly recommended.

Osteoporosis

Osteoporosis is a bone degenerative disease. These clients will usually be older people. Above all else the PT must take the client's functional capacity into consideration when training this client group. Weight-bearing activity is recommended, along with walking and jogging, although high-impact exercise is contraindicated. The PT can also implement balance training to improve the client's neuromuscular system; along with postural training this will benefit the client greatly.

Functional problems

Functional problems are anything that prevents the client from performing a particular movement or range of movement. If the client has an injury that has not been diagnosed by a physiotherapist, the PT must refer them before training them in order to ensure that the correct exercises are then programmed. Often clients who have functional problems will have notes from a physiotherapist as to what exercises are appropriate. These exercises can then be integrated into sessions in order to work towards a 'normal' functional capacity. Liaison with physiotherapists is commonplace in personal training and is mutually beneficial. The PT can even approach a physiotherapist to form a working partnership with a two-way referral system.

Some general guidelines to follow for a sample of function problems are as follows:

Lower back

Hyperlordosis: concentrate on pelvic tilts, abs and transverse abs work. Make sure that the client performs checks on their posture every day. Stretching the iliopsoas is also advised.

Muscle strains: the most common complaint that you will encounter, usually brought on by incorrect execution of daily activities. Avoid high-impact exercises and get regular feedback from the client regarding pain thresholds. You can stretch the lower back only after an appropriate warm-up.

Overall, with back problems be aware of correct posture at all times. If there is an imbalance, then you and the client can work together to correct this.

Knee

This group of conditions includes **shin splints**. These are actually micro fractures along the tibia and can be very painful. You should condition the tibialis anterior muscle and use plenty of stretching around the lower muscles, i.e. the gastrocnemius, soleus and tibialis anterior itself.

You may come across **anterior cruciate ligament** (ACL) injuries, which are the most common in footballers and players of other sports where rotation pressure is placed on the knee joint. You will need to strengthen all the muscles around the knee joint using closed chain exercises only. Depending on the degree of this injury and the stage of rehabilitation, there will probably need to be some liaison with a physiotherapist, or at least recommended exercises at hand.

Shoulder

Shoulder injuries often involve the rotator cuff muscles around the shoulder joint. You can strengthen this muscle group by using exercises such as internal and external rotation. If the client suffers from impingement at the shoulder, be wary of overhead movements and lateral raises. Focus on rhomboids, scapular and latissimus dorsi work to strengthen the whole area.

Activity 9.4

There is a wealth of information available regarding special populations. The first port of call should be the ACSM. This organisation constantly updates their position regarding each client group that you are likely to train.

Pick a random special population group and research what the ACSM recommends for training them, then seek out an alternative source that covers the same client group. There may be slight variation, but this will give you an insight into how to deal with these types of training situations.

In the case of uncertainty over special population protocols, clients need to be referred to a GP or physiotherapist, whichever is more appropriate. It is important not to proceed by trying to second guess the doctor's or physiotherapist's advice.

Reflection 9.3

Having trained many, if not all, of the client groups above, I can say that the first-hand evidence that I have witnessed is 100 per cent positive. I have trained hypertensive clients over many months and seen them lower their blood pressure and in some cases actually come off medication. My pregnant clients have all reported a positive response to training – even to the extent of most coming back post-partum to train with me further – jogging with a pram is good exercise! Weight loss clients have been amazed by what is possible from hiring a PT: significant aesthetic changes result from chronic exercising. You can have a profoundly positive affect on people who hire you.

Summary

The guidelines given in this chapter provide the basics for starting to prepare for advanced training programmes, including SAQ, plyometrics and MR. If you have a chance, explore the training equipment listed and incorporate items into your workouts in order to introduce fresh exercises. The above advice on periodisation provides a taste of what is possible in this area. Periodising programmes requires practice and patience from the PT, but the end results can be impressive for clients. Finally, taking account of special population requirements is vital to ensure safe workouts with these types of clients. If clients manifest any symptoms, it is important to seek medical advice before training them.

Further reading

Essentials of strength training and conditioning (NSCA) has been my training bible for many years and you cannot go far wrong if you adhere to the science and exercise descriptions within this book. It covers SAQ, plyometric and periodised training, and is well worth getting hold of. The ACSM text *ACSM's guidelines for exercise testing and prescription* should be an automatic purchase if you train any special population clients. It is regularly updated and contains current thinking regarding training recommendations.

ACSM (2002) *Exercise management for persons with chronic diseases and disabilities.* 2nd edition. Human Kinetics – a must-buy if you work with GP referral clients.

ACSM (2005) *ACSM's guidelines for exercise testing and prescription.* 7th edition. Lippincott Williams & Wilkins.

Baechle, T, Earle, R (2000) *Essentials of strength training and conditioning.* 2nd edition. Human Kinetics.

Bompa, T (1994) *Theory and methodology of training: the key to athletic performance.* 3rd edition. Kendall Hunt.

Chu, D (1998) *Jumping into plyometrics.* 2nd edition. Human Kinetics.

Chu, D. (2003) *Plyometric exercises with the medicine ball.* 2nd edition. Bittersweet Publishing.

Potvin, A and Jesperson, M (2004) *The great medicine ball handbook.* 3rd edition. Productive Fitness.

www.exrx.net/ExInfo/Sprint.html – general SAQ training guidelines.

www.brianmac.co.uk/plymo.htm – plyometric exercise information.

www.spinalhealth.net/plyometrics.html – this site includes links to example plyometric exercises.

www.bodyweightculture.com/ – an interesting site that advocates the use of body weight exercises.

www.pponline.co.uk/encyc/periodisation.html – a starting guide to periodising programmes.

www.brettsmith.co.nz/rugby/period.htm – a guide to periodising for rugby.

www.acsm-msse.org/ – click on the position stands link on the left to access all of the ACSM's position stands on special populations.

PART 3

Contexts

Chapter 10

Home training

The typical impression of home fitness training is of people jumping around to a 1980s Jane Fonda video. Huge numbers of fitness DVDs are sold to the general public – some well made, some downright dangerous. For PTs the benefit of these videos is that they make people aware that they can train in their own homes – and there is now also widespread awareness of the availability of PTs for home visits.

In many ways, the growth of interest in home training is a positive development for PTs: it provides opportunities for additional income and introduces variety. However, because the cost to the client of home training is greater than gym membership, by no means everyone can afford such a service.

When starting out in the profession, PTs often view the home training of clients as a daunting prospect. With only someone's living room or garden to work in, without the machines, free weights and purpose-built environment that a gym provides, what can a PT do? Clients training at home, after all, pay good money for the service, and so expect to work to the same goals and to receive the same quality of experience as in a gym. How can a PT satisfy these expectations? Until now, PTs have had to consult numerous resources – textbooks, websites, and so on – without any kind of one-stop resource. This chapter is designed to make good that lack by collating information and providing advice and creative ideas for PTs working in home settings. The chapter will therefore help you:

1. understand clients' motivations for hiring PTs to train them at home;
2. be aware of the range of equipment that is available and useful for home training;
3. make effective use of equipment;
4. understand the application of personal training codes of conduct to home training;
5. be creative in designing home training programmes.

Clients' motivations

It is useful to consider clients' motivations for hiring a PT to provide home training. These will, of course, include the general motivation to exercise. The decision specifically to hire a home trainer, however, differs in several ways from that of joining a gym. The motivation is likely to include one or more of the following factors:

1. Anxiety: a client may well be anxious, perhaps because of low self-esteem, about exercising publicly.
2. Money: if a client wants to exercise and can readily afford home training, the question for them might be, 'Why not?' rather than, 'Why?'
3. Status: having a trainer visit the client's home may be a means to display the client's disposable income.
4. Time: by removing the journey time to the gym, the total time commitment on the part of the client is reduced. The client's time can be used optimally.

In addition, clients may have experienced a *lack* of motivation to visit a gym regularly.

The sources of motivation differ between clients. Working out a client's motivation can help a PT to retain that client's custom.

Reflection 10.1

Home training clients can be quite different from gym-based clients. In some cases, I've trained clients who have never been to a gym. During the initial consultation I ask open-ended questions and encourage clients to describe what they think the sessions will entail. Within scientific guidelines, I then tailor the sessions to meet – or preferably exceed – the client's expectations. All session planning will be linked to the client's goals and will have client input and ownership. Guide rather than coerce!

Equipment

Usually, home training does not provide the range of equipment that is available in a gym. The following, however, normally are available: chairs; walls; stairs; tins of food; water (yes water!); a sofa; and doors. The question then is how to make use of these, in combination with items in the PT's own kitbag, to provide sessions that will enable clients to work towards their goals. A chair can be used for tricep dips, incline or decline press-ups, body weight squats, incline or decline lunges, or as a platform for bridges. Walls can be used for wall sits, pelvic tilts or handstand presses. Stairs have a multitude of uses, including step-ups, step-downs, cardiovascular work and calf raises.

A problem for PTs is how to transport free weights to clients' homes. A kitbag will contain light resistance equipment such as resistance bands. In addition, a number of useful items will be available in a client's house already. Tins of food may be combined inside a padded bag to provide a substitute for free weights. These may be used for almost all free weight exercises so long as safety requirements are adhered to. Tins may also be used singly as dumb-bells. A water carrier with an integral handle in the client's house or a 5-litre water bottle, once filled, can be used to provide resistance for weight training. A sofa can be used to provide a lower-leg rest for abdominal exercises. Doors can be used for chin-ups and can anchor bands for resistance exercises.

Clients' gardens can also provide a good environment. They can be useful, for example, for cardiovascular work in the warmer months of the year. Gardens may be used for shuttle runs and circuit training, with garden benches substituting for chairs.

Body weight training

A multitude of body weight exercises can be used in the home training repertoire. The following are examples:

- press-ups – and all of the different methods of performing press-ups;
- lying pull ups – you need a bar for this (use a free bar if you are strong enough to hold it in place for a client);
- squats;
- calf raises (including bilateral and unilateral);
- wall squats (these are isometric with the knees at 90 degrees);
- lunges (pulse, jumping or lateral);
- chin-ups – you need a bar for this which can be bought fairly cheaply to fit across a door frame;
- tricep dips;
- step-downs (one leg balances while the other steps down from a chair);
- handstand press (for the more athletic clients!);
- virtually all abdominal exercises;
- back extensions;
- supermans;
- plank and side planks;
- astrides – across a step.

If you consider the range of equipment and exercises available, you'll see that a wide repertoire is possible. Indeed, with careful planning, there are even more possibilities. The PT's kitbag is important here: it provides a lightweight 'gym' in itself; it makes the PT look professional, and also, with a logo on the side, provides a medium for marketing the service. If the PT is travelling by public transport, the kitbag and its contents obviously need to be kept light.

Activity 10.1

First, make a list of everything needed in a kitbag to run a varied home PT session. Then put them in order of priority. Finally, compare your list to that in the appendix at the end of this chapter.

PT's equipment: rationale

Look again at the contents listed in the appendix to this chapter. They are lightweight and will fit into a medium-sized bag. The BP monitor is essential for initial health screens and provides a necessary check when training hypertensive clients. A stopwatch and/or timer is essential, both for working to time frames within a session and for measuring total session time. The small towel is used to provide a barrier when stretching clients and in manual resistance exercises (described in Chapter 9). A training mat is necessary to keep the client comfortable when performing floor exercises.

Resistance bands provide an excellent means of resistance training for home clients. Different intensities of band tubing are available and will provide more than enough resistance for most clients (though there is the disadvantage here that the PT cannot measure the intensity).

The list of exercises for these bands is almost endless, especially if a door (DA) is used. A sample list of exercises includes:

- squats – the band is stood on by the client and the handles held by the hands in a shoulder-press position while the squat is being performed;
- wood chop (DA);
- internal/external rotation – for the shoulder (DA);
- one-arm row (DA);
- tricep pulldown and extension (DA);
- bicep curl (the band is under one foot while the exercise is being performed);
- seated row (DA);
- cable cross-over (DA);
- shoulder press (again the band is under the feet while the client presses);
- lateral raises;
- front raises;
- chest flyes – unilateral (DA);
- chest press – unilateral (DA).

Resources providing further information on resistance band exercises are listed at the end of the chapter.

A training bar can be used to provide focus when using resistance bands or performing manual resistance. Some manufacturers provide bars that break down for easy storage, though it is also possible to improvise by using, for example, a sawn-off broom. Boxing gloves are lightweight and can provide a good CV workout. (Many clients enjoy some sort of boxing training during at least some sessions – some may well want this kind of training in every session.) Skipping also provides a good CV training mode, though care needs to be taken to ensure that there is ample space. Cones can be used for various activities, including circuits and SAQ drills (see Chapter 9). The same is true of the rubber markers, which may be purchased from sports equipment suppliers. Callipers are useful for providing clients with an update on their body fat percentage. A heart rate monitor is useful during dynamic movement as it is difficult to keep palpating heart rates repeatedly – though it is advisable *always* to palpate at least one heart rate during a workout as a health screen for arrhythmias.

If a PT owns a car, this increases the range of equipment that may be carried (though it is important not to carry so much equipment that too much time is spent loading and unloading). It is useful to carry a step that includes a 'deck' for conversion into a lightweight incline bench. Adding a couple of medicine balls of different weights and a couple of body bars provides a range of light resistance equipment. A gym stability ball is also useful for a multitude of exercises. Kettle bells and resistance bags are also options. It is useful to experiment by varying the range of equipment carried.

Equipment purchased by the client

If a client wishes to purchase equipment, this can add to the range of what is available for the training sessions. The client may well ask the PT's opinion on what to buy and how to design the use of home space. This can provide a PT with an opportunity for secondary earning (for example, by ordering through the PT website, as discussed in Chapter 12). However, the PT does need to give careful consideration before providing advice. PTs have an ethical obligation not to overstretch clients financially or recommend equipment that is not appropriate to that client. The amount of space available and the clients' training goals are important criteria.

Activity 10.3

Using graph paper, plan a gym for the largest room in your home. Try using at least (a) two pieces of cardiovascular kit, (b) a bench and (c) a basic free weight set-up. Then add the smaller items such as a gym ball. Remember to include measurements of the dimensions of the room and to place the equipment with reference to the dimensions of the machines. Finally, calculate the budget required. (The fitness supplier websites listed at the end of this chapter provide information on prices.)

Ambience and space

Clients who are trained in their home have the choice of background music if they wish. It is best not to use television music channels, since television can distract clients during exercises.

It is important for the client's safety to ensure that there is sufficient light and space. It may be necessary to move furniture (with the client's consent) to provide the latter. Ceiling height is restricted in private dwellings and can cause an injury risk during jumping activities, especially with tall clients. Exercises that the PT deems too risky in the space available should never be attempted. Remember also the danger of damaging valuable objects in the client's home.

It is advisable for the PT to make a risk assessment in relation to every home training client covering all potential hazards. An example of a blank risk assessment sheet is available from **www.sahw.co.uk/main-section/workplace-topics/ risk-assessment.cfm**.

If an accident does occur, the risk assessment sheet can be used to provide evidence that the PT considered the hazards. An example of potential hazards is a lack of space to perform dynamic exercises such as plyometrics. Risk assessments are vital to the safety of clients and PTs. Because of the complexities of this subject, it is important to seek professional advice.

Activity 10.4

Draw up a risk assessment table with the following columns and complete it for your own home:

Hazard	Probability	Severity	Control measures
Detail here what could go wrong	*Indicate the likelihood of the hazard occurring*	*Indicate how serious the accident could be*	*Explain how to minimise the risk*

Professionalism

The personal trainer code of conduct is especially relevant to home training. The fact that a PT can be alone with a client in a house makes it especially important for the PT to ensure that the code of conduct is adhered to. The REPs code states, for example: 'Ensure that physical contact is appropriate and necessary and is carried out within recommended guidelines and with the participant's full consent and approval. Demonstrate proper personal behaviour and conduct at all times.'

PTs can receive unwanted advances from clients and need to protect themselves from this kind of attention. Though it may seem flattering, the consequences can be serious – especially if the client is attached or overly needy (or both!). As a professional, the PT must either drop the person from the list of clients or be sure to manage the situation carefully. The REPs code states: 'Avoid sexual intimacy with clients while instructing, or immediately after a training session, and . . . arrange to transfer the client to another professional if it is clear that an intimate relationship is developing.' Care is required because the PT has a legal duty of care. If a relationship is developing in an unhealthy manner, the PT needs to cease providing the client with a service.

It is important to have a dress code for PT and client. The PT needs always to look professional, wearing, for example, a clean polo shirt with logo and either long shorts or loose-fitting trousers. The client should be dressed appropriately in gym wear or loose-fitting clothing and training shoes.

Creativity

The key to home training is creativity. PTs must use their exercise depth charts to maximum effect. Home training is an art that requires numerous sessions to perfect. The initial consultation with the client provides an opportunity to work out which exercises will and will not be possible. The PT can explore the space available and also find out which home items are available for use as equipment, as discussed above. Collecting this information before the first training session will save time and also emphasise the PT's professionalism. Combining the home equipment with body weight exercises, plyometrics, SAQ training, circuit training, manual resistance and exercises using kitbag equipment provides a vast array of possibilities.

Reflection 10.2

*One piece of equipment that is inexpensive and lightweight, and that may be utilised in a home environment consists of two discs that slide across surfaces with your client standing on them. These can be used to good effect during body weight exercises and even some cardiovascular workouts. Another recent development, particularly popular in the USA, is called suspension training. The kit involves a strap with either a door or wall anchor combined with handles and foot straps. The client uses their body weight to perform many different exercises – it really is a home gym and may well take home PT by storm in the UK. It is light, portable and adaptable. See **www.personaltraining1st.com** for further information on this piece of kit and UK availability.*

Activity 10.5

Draw up two programmes for a client as if you were going to train them in your home. Try something straightforward initially, such as 10 body weight exercises in a circuit session. Then try working on a programme for a client who wants hypertrophy using a split routine over three days per week. Note that the second programme will be more challenging, but you should be able to use manual resistance here effectively. Once you have your programmes, ask a friend or family member to volunteer to be trained by you so that you can try the exercises in the order you have programmed.

If you are an experienced PT, you need to think laterally and explore new and innovative equipment or different ways of using this equipment. Remember the importance of keeping your client interested and motivated, which can be more difficult in their home surroundings.

Activity 10.6

Assemble all your kit together with the typical home items used in training. As in Chapter 7, develop a written list of all the home exercises that you use. Try then to research and develop some additional exercises and surf the Internet to see what new equipment is available. Practise the exercises yourself. This activity should be conducted at least twice per year to ensure that you keep developing your home training repertoire.

Summary

This chapter has emphasised that there is usually a wealth of equipment in clients' homes that may, with a little creativity, be used for personal training. A PT who begins to acquire home clients needs also to develop a kitbag with equipment for a variety of exercises. PTs should practise exercises themselves in order to learn how to use the equipment effectively and to develop their creativity. PTs involved in home training must adhere to the code of conduct for PTs and protect themselves from litigation wherever possible. Home training clients are often the best source of income for most PTs: building a home client-base and continuing to develop professionally can lead to career success.

Further study

Few PT texts deal with home training at all, although you may find some of the home training books aimed at the general public useful. One example is:

Wolff, R (2002) *Home bodybuilding: three easy steps to building your body and changing your life.* Adams Media Corp. This book explores home training from the client's point of view.

The best advice is to build your exercise lists from this chapter and then explore the links below to enhance your knowledge base:

http://exercise.about.com/od/resistancebandworkouts/Resistance_Band_Workouts. htm – this website covers many resistance band exercises with many illustrations;
www.performbetter.com/catalog/assets/Exercisesheets/PDF/MedBall%20Handou t.pdf – examples of medicine ball exercises;
www.exerciseregister.org/custom/REPsInformationGuidance.htm – the REPs website that includes documents such as the code of conduct mentioned in this chapter;
www.personaltraining1st.com – this site will provide links for various UK equipment suppliers for sourcing equipment for your kitbags and clients' homes.

Appendix: Contents list for kitbag for home training

Blood pressure monitor
Stopwatch/timer (can be on a wristwatch)
Small towel
Training mat
Resistance bands
Latex bands
Suspension training straps
Training bar
Boxing gloves and mitts
Skipping rope
Cones
Rubber markers
Callipers (percentage BF)
Heart rate monitor

Chapter 11

Health fitness trainer

In this chapter we consider the role of 'health trainers' with regard to the National Health Service (NHS) in the UK. Encouraging physical activity has, along with healthy eating, become a key objective of health policy. For prospective PTs, the hope is that future UK governments will invest *properly* in physical activity schemes that employ or hire fitness professionals to help tackle health problems.

This chapter focuses in particular on the problem of obesity. The campaign against obesity has come to the forefront of health policy. This is for good reasons: obesity is associated with increased risk of a wide array of health problems. Initiatives designed to counter the rise of obesity have therefore become high profile.

The author considers the development of links between PTs and the general populace through GP referral schemes and future government directives to be paramount in the fight against obesity. If such initiatives develop, the personal training sector will grow and new entrants to the profession will be well placed to benefit.

This chapter is designed to help you to:

1. acquire knowledge about health problems in the UK, especially obesity;
2. understand the role of the health trainer;
3. recognise that there are GP referral schemes that provide work opportunities already;
4. be aware of what qualifications are required to work in this sector;
5. formulate a view on future trends and how to benefit from them as a PT.

The case of obesity

In the UK obesity levels are staggering. Official statistics indicate that obesity has risen by 38 per cent in the general population since 2003 and that by 2010, on current trends, one-third of men will be obese, as will 19 per cent of boys and 22 per cent of girls aged 2–15. In contrast, in the 1980s only 6 per cent of the UK population was classed as obese (see, for example, **http://news.bbc.co.uk/1/hi/health/5277350.stm**). At current rates of growth, by 2050, 50 per cent of women and 60 per cent of men will be obese. Obesity is associated with health risks – diabetes, coronary disease and strokes in particular. On these figures, by 2050 the incidence of type 2 diabetes would rise by 70 per cent, coronary disease by 20 per cent and strokes by 30 per cent.

The cost

In 2002, the NHS in the UK spent £7 billion on treating health problems that were experienced by overweight or obese patients. Cost projections are unsustainable: by 2047 the cost of obesity will rise to £46 billion (at current UK prices). The NHS will not be able to cope with costs of this magnitude. There is, of course, also a human cost. An obese person has an average life expectancy of nearly nine years less than someone with normal weight and body fat. In 2004, the Department of Health estimated that people who take regular physical activity are 20–30 per cent less likely to exhibit premature mortality and 50 per cent less at risk of experiencing heart disease, strokes, diabetes and cancer.

This is a sobering thought for the huge numbers of sedentary people in the UK – or so you would think. In fact, most people *know* that physical activity leads to health, yet according to government statistics, 70 per cent of adults, 30 per cent of boys and 40 per cent of girls miss the 'five exercise periods per week' target recommended by the UK's Chief Medical Officer (CMO). (See **www.dh.gov.uk/en/Publicationsand statistics/Publications/PublicationsPolicyAndGuidance/DH_4080994**.) Figure 11.1 shows a graphical representation of the situation.

As is clear from the diagram, there is a large group of adults who do not commit to regular physical activity – those who 'do not, but can'. This group needs targeting through increased intervention from fitness professionals. We need to remember the

Figure 11.1: Individual activity levels in the UK (based on CMO data, 2004)

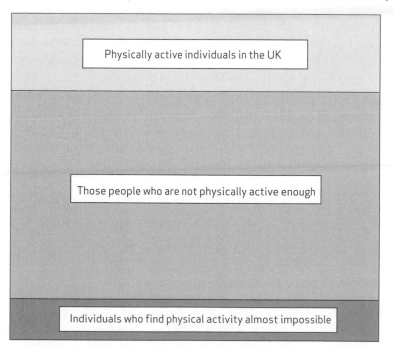

adage that 'prevention is better than cure'. This section of the population requires intervention *before* they exhibit symptoms of disease. Just think of all the GP referrals and potential clients that could result from preventative policies!

Why does this section of the population not take regular exercise? Many people do not exercise regularly because they either do not wish to or have lacked an impetus to want to start. Therefore, this 'do not, but can' section of the population can be subdivided, with those people who are more willing to exercise placed in the 'impetus' category. It is not possible to say exactly how many people fall into each subdivision, but the sheer overall numbers involved – over 60 million people live in the UK – must make this group worth targeting.

The NHS health trainer

In 2006, the first cohort of health trainers were dispatched by the NHS to help tackle the growing health problems within lower socio-economic communities in the UK. The initial 88 primary care trusts that hired and trained these health trainers were to be followed in 2007 by the rest of the country. The health trainers' primary goals are to advise, motivate and provide practical support to those individuals who would like to adopt healthier lifestyles.

Trainers were to be recruited from the local community to appeal to the target audience. They were encouraged to work one-to-one with their 'clients' in a similar way to PTs. Their remit is to tackle the key areas for actions outlined in the government white paper entitled 'Choosing Health' (2004). These include smoking, sexual health, drinking, obesity and general overall health. Health trainers work with health promotion strategies and psychological interventions that target these problem areas.

The training that health trainers receive in some NHS trusts lasts a minimum of three months, after which they take modules to acquire specific knowledge regarding the particular needs of their community. Another route into the health trainer discipline is via the City & Guilds level 3 Certificate for Health Trainers qualification, which is available in increasing numbers of training centres across the UK.

The concept of health trainers has been adopted too by the UK armed forces, with the army training their PT instructors in the health promotion techniques needed to increase soldiers' general health. Hopefully, then, the occupation of health trainer is gaining acceptance in the UK. The link between health trainers and personal trainers could be developed to allow specialist 'Health Fitness Trainers' (HFT) to be created. If you are interested in pursuing this, you are recommended to contact local GP surgery exercise referral schemes.

Activity 11.1

Perform an Internet search to see if there are health trainer initiatives being run in your area. Research the salaries offered and consider the possibility of adding this area of expertise to your own PT skill base.

GP referral schemes

The practice of GPs referring patients to local leisure centres for exercise programmes has been developing over the last decade. This reflects GPs' greater awareness of the benefits of physical activity and use of exercise as prescriptive 'medicine' to treat a number of conditions. The health areas that feature prominently here are hypertension, diabetes, cancer, mental health, physical rehabilitation and obesity. There are two obstacles that slow the rate of growth of these schemes: first, a lack of sufficient trust or understanding of the fitness industry and, second, the influence of drug companies and their sales reps (if a patient is referred to a gym, the demand for drugs will fall). Nevertheless, it seems inevitable that the referral system will continue to grow: the government will not increase its funding of the NHS indefinitely and the drugs often treat only symptoms rather than cure the underlying disease. An example is hypertension: beta-blockers will lower a patient's heart rate and therefore lower their blood pressure (with side effects) as long as the patient takes the drug; if, on the other hand, patients lowered their blood pressure by means of chronic exercise, their blood pressure would be lower due to the reduction of fatty deposits in the vascular system, thus lowering the total peripheral resistance to the blood being pumped by the heart. The benefit would remain so long as the patients continued to exercise. An additional benefit is that the side effects from exercise are positive. They include the reduced risk of other diseases developing and the increased functional capacity of the patient.

How is a GP referral scheme structured? A typical model would follow the sequence below:

1. The patient visits a GP with a health problem.
2. The GP refers the patient for exercise prescription (usually at a local leisure facility).
3. The patient's first visit to the leisure centre involves an initial consultation, fitness testing and motivational advice.
4. The sessions themselves typically number up to 20 over two months.
5. After these sessions have been monitored, the patient will receive an exit fitness test and exercise counselling.
6. The patient revisits the GP for evaluation.
7. Where appropriate, the patient is redirected to the leisure centre (at a reduced membership rate) in order to increase exercise adherence.
8. There is a further, less regular, monitoring to ensure long-term adherence.

Activity 11.2

What do you think are the potential problems with the model above? Critique each step in the patient's journey and then propose ways to improve the process with reference to the use of exercise professionals.

Activity 11.3

1. Research the ways in which regular chronic exercise can positively affect patients at risk from coronary disease, diabetes, hypertension and obesity.
2. Research the number of local GP surgeries near you that use exercise referral schemes. This could be done by visiting the surgeries and explaining that you are a student who is researching the likelihood of local patients being referred to a fitness facility.

Evaluation of exercise referral schemes

In March 2007, the Department of Health (DH) issued best practice guidance to primary care trusts on the use of exercise referral schemes (DH *Statement on exercise referral*). It recommended:

- targeting type 2 diabetes, obesity and osteoporosis;
- adherence for such schemes to the National Quality Assurance Framework for exercise referral in England;
- that GPs should promote the minimum of 30 minutes of moderate activity on at least five days per week as a preventative measure for the general population;
- promoting schemes to asymptomatic people only when 'these are part of a properly designed and controlled research study to determine effectiveness'.

The DH commissioned the National Institute for Health and Clinical Excellence (NICE) to research the effectiveness of exercise referral schemes. Results suggested a positive effect on physical activity rates in the short term (6–12 weeks of adherence), though problems arose with lower adherence rates over longer time periods. (The author suggests that this fall in adherence rates over the longer term may be associated with insufficient investment in PT involvement after the first twelve weeks of patient attendance.)

Activity 11.4

It is useful here to consider what more can be done to stem the rising tide of obesity and the impact of sedentary lifestyles on the population's health. As a potential participant in the solution, what strategies could you suggest?

1. Construct a list of three goals that you believe the DH should focus on over the next 10 years. Make them simple. They could relate to obesity, heart disease or diabetes.
2. Brainstorm two of these strategies to involve PTs that could be implemented to help achieve these UK health goals, bearing in mind budgetary constraints.
3. Now choose one of your strategies and develop this into a brief plan for implementation. Compare this to, and critique, the author's ideas below.

Reflection 11.1

I have visited various NHS departments in the south east of England and studied many physical activity health promotion strategies. Such strategies are not determined by the opinions of fitness professionals. Rather, they are determined by financial constraints and the opinions of other professionals. The NHS published a document Learning from Local Exercise Action Pilots (LEAP) *that summarised conclusions drawn from data from 10 different exercise intervention projects delivered by NHS trusts, GPs, local authorities, schools, community groups and sports clubs during 2003–2005. The report looked at short-term changes in 10,433 participants' activity levels in four activity level categories and found an overall median increase in brisk walking of 75 minutes per week. It concluded that 'LEAP interventions were cost effective to implement' and 'demonstrated that the potential cost savings to the National Health Service exceeded the costs per participant of implementing the intervention'. Two of the report's main recommendations were to use 'trained and skilled staff' and a 'tailored approach', i.e. an individual approach to exercise prescription.*

At the time of the LEAP pilots, a report by the CMO At least five a week: Evidence on the impact of physical activity and its relationship to health *(DH, 2004) looked at evidence from strategies that promote 'moderate intensity' activity, and found that walking, in particular, increased physical activity adherence.*

Two questions arise from these studies. First, where are the commercial PTs in the set up? The commercial PT sector is virtually ignored in government discussion of health promotion. Second, is 'brisk walking' the term most applicable to the search for optimum health gains? Walking can certainly improve the health of totally sedentary people, but any talk of walking as some sort of health panacea is problematic. (Consider, for example, target heart rate zones when programming exercise for PT clients.) There needs to be clarification of the role and terminology concerning moderate intensity and brisk walking. In the PT arena we usually talk about moderate intensity as equating to around 70 per cent MHR (for example, a 30-year-old client might have to work at 133 BPM to achieve that low-end THRZ). Would brisk walking elicit that response in most 30-year-olds? I think it would not. So is brisk walking a good indicator for producing health-related fitness gains? You decide.

Skills for working with clients with health issues

What skills are required to enter and work effectively in the health sector in the UK?

A minimum requirement is the level 2 gym instructor award (NVQ or VRQ – see Chapter 12). This will allow the holder to work in any UK fitness facility as a gym instructor. Currently in the UK there is no health and fitness qualification to match the ACSM Health Fitness Instructor (HFI). The ACSM are the world specialists when it comes to health and the implementation of exercise to decrease disease and increase prevention of disease. The NHS in the UK would do well either to take the ACSM as a standard or to base a UK health fitness trainer on the ACSM model. The HFI qualification does at least demonstrate that the holder has acquired knowledge to deal with the health sector. There are level 3 PT courses run by various training providers. It is best to pick one that is internationally recognised. All these courses can be studied alongside degree courses and provide students with a head start after graduation. For people who already have a level 3 REPs qualification, there are private training companies that offer level 4 REPs qualifications covering work with clients with health issues such as obesity, ageing, mental health, low back pain and heart disease. There are other requisites for this level 4 status and it is worth visiting **www.exerciseregister.org/custom/documents/L4QualificationArrangementFinal.pdf** for an up-to-date description of the requirements of this level 4 status.

PTs who gain experience in working with special population clients will make themselves more marketable, especially in the health sector. It is possible, for example, to offer your services for short work experience periods with specialist NHS units such as local cardiac rehab units. It is also possible to qualify as a level 3 health trainer through City & Guilds, which provides specific health promotion knowledge. A trainer with ACSM HFI and a City & Guilds Certificate for Health Trainers would be an asset in any physical activity government strategy.

Future trends and opportunities for PTs

The UK government needs to invest in professional health fitness trainers to augment the work of health trainers. This may well provide a career path offering a salary above the level currently earned by health trainers. Imagine the potential impact of a team of professional health fitness trainers in the local community targeting the 'can do, but will not' section of the population. The government's own evidence has indicated that exercise adherence only lasts around 2–3 months and that one of the 'categories for best practice in the UK' is the targeted individual approach, which PTs could provide by working on a one-to-one basis with clients who exhibit specific health issues. The PT sector in the UK is growing at a fast rate, so there is a supply of trainers available. Although the NHS could not afford to pay trainers the commercial single session rate for a client, PTs could be prepared to provide a block of sessions at a lower rate, especially in quieter periods in their schedule. All sides might benefit: the community would gain a service provided by professional PTs and the PT would gain opportunities to market their own services (through, for example, word-of-mouth publicity). This model would also allow the NHS and PT sectors to communicate effectively in the pursuit of the same goal, namely, an increase in the number of people in the UK who exercise regularly.

You may have altruistic feelings towards the community you live and work in. Remember that there are GP referral schemes running in local leisure centres and other community exercise initiatives, so there are already opportunities to make a contribution that you can research to see what is taking place in your local area. The health area is a growing market that will need future investment by the government if the targets for reducing obesity and levels of disease are to be met. Nobody can be sure how this sector will develop, but it is sensible for PTs to consider possible career paths.

Activity 11.5

Draw up a list of the potential advantages and disadvantages to the PT of working with GP referrals. Plan a career path, including (a) qualifications and (b) experience that would allow you to take advantage of opportunities in this area.

Summary

Having studied this chapter you should be in no doubt over the seriousness of the problem of obesity and related health problems in the UK. The UK's health bodies are in agreement concerning the benefits of exercise for the population as a whole. The benefits of intervention in the area of physical activity and exercise are well documented. The development of the health trainer role in the NHS is a relatively new initiative designed to reduce the incidence of disease in local communities. If this role is professionally developed and supported with investment, intervention may have a greater impact on the nation's health. This chapter has outlined the development of GP referral schemes and examined how they relate to the role of PTs in the community and also the potential impact on the market for PTs. The qualifications needed to work in the health sector can be wide-ranging and PTs must gain relevant certification in order to work safely with special populations and health clients. The precise future of the role of health fitness trainers is uncertain. Much depends on the extent to which the government recognises the need to include professional, well remunerated, PTs in its exercise strategies. Without that, the figures for effective intervention are likely to remain modest. If, however, the health service trusts the fitness industry's experience in the health arena, the possibilities for future intervention are bright.

Further reading

At the time of writing there is no textbook written specifically for health trainers in the UK. The following ACSM publications provide the definitive guides to training health clients and are must-haves for prospective PTs in this field:

ACSM (2005) *ACSM's guidelines for exercise testing and prescription.* 7th edition. Lippincott Williams & Wilkins.
ACSM (2007) *Resources for the personal trainer.* 2nd edition. Lippincott Williams & Wilkins.

In addition, the following books and websites provide helpful information:

Howley, F (2007) *Fitness professional's handbook.* 5th edition. Human Kinetics.
Lawrence, D (2006) *GP referral schemes, working with referred clients.* A & C Black.

www.nice.org.uk/nicemedia/pdf/PH002_physical_activity.pdf is the report from NICE that outlines the recommendations mentioned in the chapter. The document also contains links to other resources.

www.dh.gov.uk/en/Publichealth/Healthimprovement/Healthyliving/LocalExerciseActionPilotsLEAP/index.htm accesses the DH publication *Learning from LEAP.* This summary document is based on the final report by Leeds Metropolitan University on the LEAP programme pilots: *The national evaluation of LEAP* (2007), which can be found at

www.dh.gov.uk/en/Publicationsandstatistics/Publications/PublicationsPolicyAndGuidance/DH_073600

www.dh.gov.uk/en/Publicationsandstatistics/Publications/PublicationsPolicyAndGuidance/DH_4080994 for the CMO's 2004 report *At least five a week: Evidence on the impact of physical activity and its relationship to health.*

www.networks.nhs.uk/uploads/06/03/health_trainers_aug05.pdf is a review of the first cohort of health trainers.

www.bradfordairedale-pct.nhs.uk/Our+Services/health+trainers/ is an example of a successful health trainer initiative.

www.city-and-guilds.co.uk/cps/rde/xchg/cgonline/hs.xsl/18743.html gives details of the City & Guilds health trainer qualification.

www.networks.nhs.uk/networks.php?pid=29 is the NHS health trainer resource page.

www.nwph.net/champs/Publications/Forms/DispForm.aspx?ID=27
A health trainer's training pack is available from this site.

Chapter 12

Business sense

People entering the fitness industry sometimes forget that it is a business like any other. You may well seek a job in the industry because you enjoy being involved with fitness, health and sport. That should not, however, deflect your attention from the business factors involved. PTs need to understand not only training techniques and the science that underlies them, but also business practice. Commercially successful PTs will have developed strong business acumen themselves or have a strong team behind them to develop the business.

The most usual route is to begin working in house (employed by a gym) and then, as your skills develop, to start training external clients. In this case, the PT needs to develop entrepreneurial and sales skills as well as training skills.

This chapter is designed to help you understand:

1. how to break into the industry;
2. how the industry operates;
3. how to develop personal training client bases;
4. the need to target niche client markets;
5. how to market a personal training business;
6. how to begin business planning.

Starting in the industry

How do you start personal training? The first step is certification: you must be qualified in order to train your clients safely. In the UK, the usual way to become a PT is to get a job as a gym instructor and work your way into PT at your gym. This is a tried and tested method that works in many ways. You get experience of training clients as well as networking with other PTs to gain knowledge of the industry. In order to gain employment as a gym instructor you will need to complete at least a VRQ or NVQ qualification at level 2 in order to apply for entry on the Register of Exercise Professionals. NVQs (National Vocational Qualification) involve 'on the job' training with teaching and assessment in the workplace, while VRQs (Vocationally Related Qualification) are designed as workplace preparation (and may include some 'work experience'). Qualifications are designed by a number of awarding bodies, for example, CYQ (Central YMCA Qualifications). The website **www.leisureopportunities.co.uk** is well worth exploring. It provides a list of training providers in the UK. There is likely to be a training provider near you. You may also consult your local colleges about their courses.

Once you have achieved your level 2 qualification you can start to think about other certification pathways into personal training. Make the most of any in-house training courses supplied by the gym where you work, as these are usually provided free of charge. If a course is offered, take it: even if you will not use the information soon, you may benefit in the future. Various training organisations offer level 3 or higher degree courses in fitness and in some cases specific personal training courses.

The personal training business in the UK

Let's start with some facts and figures. In 2006 the UK health and fitness sector was valued at £2.5 billion, having grown by 4 per cent in the preceding year. Some 90 per cent of the UK population lives within 2 miles of a fitness facility. There are approximately 40,000 trained fitness professionals in the industry. In 2006 the National Fitness Audit found that:

- there were 1,671,451 members in UK gyms;
- 53 per cent were female and 47 per cent male;
- almost half were less than 35 years old;
- a significant number were high achievers in full-time employment;
- 66 per cent did not have children.

These figures provide a snapshot of the industry. There seems to be plenty of opportunity and growth, but there are also limitations because of the difficulty of attracting new exercisers. There may also be a downturn in numbers if the economy experiences recession. Nevertheless, the UK fitness industry is well worth exploring as a career path.

Overall in the UK, fitness facilities fall into four sectors: (a) commercial (large gym chains), (b) corporate (in-house business gyms), (c) local authority (pre-dominately leisure centres) and (d) stand-alone (small, privately owned) health clubs. The differences between these can be stark: gym fees can vary from £30 per month in some local authority gyms to over £100 for a basic service in flagship commercial gyms. Service levels vary accordingly. In flagship gyms, for example, clients will receive a complimentary towel and be able to use spa facilities and a frequently updated range of equipment. A local authority centre, on the other hand, may provide little more than a basic gym plus shower facilities. Corporate gyms are less well known. The gym may be incorporated into the building where their employees work. The corporate sector has grown significantly in recent years and is worth exploring as a potential employer. Due to the consolidation of the fitness industry in the UK there are fewer stand-alone gyms operating. These find it difficult to compete with the large chains. They usually try to do so by providing a distinctive service, usually based on a social model. They can operate on a more personal basis as they tend to have smaller client bases to manage. Stand-alone gyms often try to make the experience they offer more of a social event by promoting friendly, approachable staff and member interaction.

Reflection 12.1

I started in a small hospital gym, then moved to a very large urban gym that had many thousands of members, and then went into the corporate sector, training high earners in Canary Wharf in central London. I then moved within the same company to another site in the City of London where I was a fitness manager, providing personal training in-house and externally. Experience has taught me that each type of gym has its pros and cons.

I recommend attending as many interviews as possible when you are starting out. The healthiest way to approach interviews is to remember that you are interviewing the gym as well as the gym finding out about you! Find out:

- what training do they offer?
- what promotion possibilities might there be?
- how can you increase your salary?
- what remuneration method do they use?
- what budget, if any, is there for external training courses?

If there is a limited number of gyms where you live, you could always ask to visit them rather than waiting to apply for a job opportunity. Many gyms will be happy to show you around if you say you are thinking of entering the industry and some may even offer a couple of days' work experience. Interviews and visits will prove invaluable when deciding who to work for.

There are many employment and remuneration models in the UK personal training industry. Methods vary between even the large players, such as Virgin Active, Fitness First, LA Fitness and Cannons. Examples of in-house methods include the following:

1. Salaried – the PT gets paid a fixed salary no matter how many sessions they commit to.
2. 50:50 – the trainer works as a gym instructor for a set time (say, 20 hours per week) and then uses the rest of the time to provide personal training. The PT receives a pro rata salary for the 20 hours of gym instructing and then gets paid per PT session on top of this.
3. Contracted – the gym allows an external PT company to train clients in their gym. The contractor pays a fixed fee to the gym for the privilege.
4. Individual renting – external PTs can rent gym space per client. This is a favoured method in the hotel gym industry.
5. In-house PT – the trainer works for the gym and take a percentage per session conducted.

The best advice when seeking employment is to shop around to find the best offers. Basic salaries for gym instructors in the UK are low. Most gym instructors quickly decide that the area in which to make money is personal training. Many head into this arena, while some leave the industry altogether.

Starting your own business

This section is designed to provide a starting point for setting up your own personal training business. Please note that it focuses on aspects relating specifically to personal training businesses. Clearly, it is not possible here to provide a more comprehensive guide to setting up businesses in general. You are strongly advised, therefore, to use the material below in conjunction with other resources. One particularly helpful, informative and wide-ranging resource is Business Link (**www.businesslink.gov.uk**). It provides a one-stop resource covering such areas as insurance, taxation, financial issues, health and safety requirements, data protection, general legal matters and business structure.

Here we focus on market research, business planning and marketing.

Market research

Consider what you need to discover about your potential clients. It is useful to research their likely income levels and their demographic profile. It is a fact that more affluent areas will have a higher concentration of potential clients – though of course there is likely to be more competition from other PTs in those areas. Competition is not necessarily a problem: you just need to be better than your competitors! Remember that word-of-mouth communication between clients and potential clients is still a very powerful form of marketing. If you offer something different in a professional manner, you can start to establish yourself as an external self-employed PT.

You can begin to research an area simply by walking around, observing the types of housing and people. It is useful then to access some online statistics. The government provides statistics at **www.statistics.gov.uk/** Click on the neighbourhood link at the top and enter the postcode and size of area you want data for and you will find you can access a wide range of datasets. The sorts of data that will prove useful include socio-economic status and occupational groups, which will indicate the overall potential for higher earners in your catchment area.

When you have decided on a suitable area, it is important to look at the type of clients involved. Factors such as their age, gender and parental status will all be important.

> ### Activity 12.1
>
> Make a list of some potential client groups that you can identify in your local area. Examples might include: seniors; families; pregnant women; sport-specific clients; and wedding clients. Remember not to discount specialist client groups. There can be untapped markets in certain areas. For example,

Activity 12.1 continued

white collar boxing is popular among city workers. If you have experience of boxing, you could market yourself as a specialist boxing PT. There may be an opportunity among post-natal groups, where you could train small groups of women with their prams and buggies in the local park – a great idea to get them back into shape! This would provide a great marketing tool, combining primary goals with the social aspect of training in groups.

You could even aim for the highest profile clients of all – celebrities. Though this market is difficult to break into, sometimes all that is needed is to be associated with one celebrity client and business will grow from there. The key is not to ignore potential income streams. Your marketing efforts, however, must be targeted towards specific client groups and you may want to use different strategies for different client groups.

Competitors

Once you have an idea of where you want to build your business and the list of PTs operating in that area, it is useful to find out:

- the types of service they offer;
- their prices;
- the size and locations of the businesses – for example, are they operating out of a plush health club or training home clients?
  The easiest way to find this out is simply to phone them.

Activity 12.2

Visit **www.statistics.gov.uk/,** go to 'neighbourhood' and type in your postcode to research the area in which you live. If you think that there are not enough high earners in this district, try a postcode for what you consider to be a promising area. Next, research the competition using **www.yell.com** (where you can search for personal trainers by postcode) or **www.exerciseregister.org/** Also try performing a general Internet search for PTs' websites using a search engine such as **www.google.co.uk**.

Business planning

Whether you are already serious about starting a business at some point or would just like to explore the idea, it is helpful to start to draft a business plan, accompanied by a checklist of actions required. A properly thought-out business plan would, of course, be needed if you were applying to a bank or other lender for start-up finance.

Building on your business ideas so far in this chapter, start to develop a business plan. Follow these guidelines. More detailed notes on some of the following points are provided later in this section.

1. Acquire a project book (any book or file that can be divided into sections).
2. On the first page, enter your business name and logo design.
3. On the next page, write your mission statement.
4. Include a SWOT analysis, i.e. an analysis of the strengths, weaknesses, opportunities and threats relating to your proposed business. An excellent free template for this sheet is available from **www.businessballs.com/freematerialsinword/free_SWOT_analysis_temp late.doc.**
5. Next, define and explain your specific market. A couple of pages should suffice. The explanation should include PT sector trends, current industry position and prospective customer profiles. Your client demographic and PT competition searches can go here.
6. Use the next section to explain what services you will be offering and how they sit within the current market in your chosen catchment area. Explain why your business has a good chance of success.
7. Include a financial projection, showing projected revenue, costs and profits/losses. Costs will include equipment (including depreciation), clothing, transport, marketing, insurance, stationery and IT resources, accountancy and legal services.
8. Use the next section for information and ideas about marketing. For example, place your draft brochures, newsletters, press releases and website ideas here.
9. The final section is for appendices such as reports, statistics or documents that are relevant to your business plan.

Though the above exercise does not provide a fully fledged business plan, it does provide the starting point for such a plan. This can be converted into a professional plan using advice and formats available from a number of sources, including Business Link, your local banks and websites such as **www.bplans.co.uk**. Remember that a business plan needs constantly to be reviewed and updated.

Name and logo

Avoid using words in your business name that will limit your potential client bases, as you may want to expand your base in the future to include other client groups. Look for something recognisable but not cheesy. The most commonly used words include body, fitness, health and training.

Activity 12.4

Brainstorm a new business name for your PT company. The best method is to get a few friends together and ask them to help. It can be surprising how people who do not know the industry will have ideas that are catchy. Then design a logo using your business name at **www.logomaker.com/**. Ensure the design is simple and will not date quickly.

Mission statements

Write a statement based on who you are, what you will do and who you will do it for. The statement should be brief and easily understood by your potential customers. Keep it flexible and use it to make your business stand out from the crowd. Guidance is available from **www.mystrategicplan.com/strategic-planning-topics/mission-statements.shtml,** which provides advice on how to start your mission statement using single words and then build the statement from there.

Involving other people

Networking is extremely important, both for telling other people about the business and for finding people who may be able to contribute one way or another.

Reflection 12.2

Sometimes the best networking opportunity comes from a chance meeting with another professional. It may not be another PT or fitness industry professional; it may be an accountant or local business person. Treat everyone you meet in a professional manner and exchange business cards with them for future reference. Trade fairs are excellent places to chat with suppliers of equipment and meet other trainers. Seminars and conferences are great for networking as you can strike up conversations with other PTs and other people in the industry and discover mutual business interests. Always be prepared for networking opportunities and carry some business cards with you.

Activity 12.5

Online networking can be very rewarding. Try joining a discussion board or PT website and then post questions or general PT threads in order to build up a list of contacts. For example, you can visit **http://pt1st.proboards105.com/index.cgi** and post your details to allow other PTs to discuss possible PT problems and solutions with you.

You may also wish to find a mentor, for example, an experienced PT. Sometimes it is possible to reward them by providing some form of help

Marketing your business

Marketing is a discipline in its own right. This section can deal with the basics with specific regard to personal training. It is important to know which groups you are going to target in your marketing. Different groups respond to different cues. The nature of the group you are targeting will affect everything about your marketing campaign – the use of language, choice of brand colours, and so on. Also bear in mind the importance of referrals from personal acquaintances of yours – friends, work colleagues and family. Word of mouth will usually bring more clients than any other method.

Activity 12.6

Choose a potential target client group. Produce a draft A4 brochure that can be folded in three to give you six panels of information (back and front). Use the type of images, colours and text that you think will target this group. If you find that you struggle for inspiration, try looking at some websites – not necessarily PT websites – aimed at the client group. Consider their use of images, language, design and so forth. Remember that clients' *perception* is all-important here.

Marketing on a budget

It is important not to overstretch your marketing budget. Advertising may be costly and will not necessarily bring much return. There are many other ways to market your business. Here is a selection.

1. Offer trial sessions (perhaps shorter than the usual session time); be careful not to offer more than one free session.
2. Using web marketing. A PT in the UK needs a website. This may not be for primary marketing, but when a potential client hears of your services, it does provide a means of looking you up.
3. Produce a newsletter. These can be more effective than brochures if they have articles that the potential client wants to read. Make sure to have your contact details written large and clear on these.
4. Provide a free seminar. You can give the seminar an attractive title such as 'build a six pack' and 'drop a dress size'.

5. Guerrilla marketing: this involves making use of anything that has your brand or particularly your website printed on it. A host of promotional items is available for you to get printed with your business name on them. Be sure you choose something *relevant*, such as a gym bag, t-shirt, pedometer or gym towel. Be aware that many companies have minimum orders for these items.

6. Issue a press release. This is a news story that you send to a news editor of a local publication. This provides 'free' advertising for your business, but only if the editor is convinced that your story is newsworthy. You can increase the chances of this by focusing the story on a topical subject such as obesity. For instance, if you started training GP referral patients from a local GP surgery, this would be applicable. Press releases should follow a set format. You can look up an example at **www.bizhelp24.com/marketing/press-release-example.html**.

7. Provide testing offers: you offer to give a free fitness test of a particular aspect of a potential client's fitness. (If you are offering a body fat percentage test, do not use callipers as this would take too long. Use body fat scales instead.) Use the opportunity to inform the client about your services.

8. Gain referrals: link yourself to another business and have a two-way referral process. These businesses can include physiotherapists, health food stores, weight loss clubs and beauty salons.

You may also want to produce printed marketing materials. Collect examples of printed material from other PTs in your area. Use any brochures you produce to back up your business by supporting marketing and sales contacts you have made, rather than being sent out 'cold' to all and sundry. Flyers can be useful too, especially if they are vibrant, use laymen's language and are used to promote special offers.

With all forms of marketing you should keep a record of what works best and concentrate on that form of marketing with your business. The best marketing should use a mixture of 'rational' and 'irrational' appeal (rational approaches appeal to people's logic and provide information; irrational forms are aimed at their feelings and emotions).

Activity 12.7

1. Produce a newsletter that targets your client group. Use articles that will appeal to them. Include your contact details.
2. Write a sample press release for your local paper. Make it relevant to a current news story or to a new initiative you are launching that will benefit the local community. Use a standard press release format.

Web marketing

You will need to have a website and email address if you want to be taken seriously as a business. Many potential clients will want to look up information on your business before deciding whether to hire you. The great thing about web-based marketing is that you are open 24 hours a day, seven days a week for information.

Unless you have a good knowledge base regarding the building of websites, website development can be costly. Note that you have a choice between hiring a web designer, which provides you with flexibility to produce a purpose-designed site, or using an online website builder, which tends to cost less, but involves design constraints.

Activity 12.8

Check out other PTs' websites by performing an Internet search for your local area. You will find variations in the tone, design and depth of PT websites. Decide which ones you think have the right balance of selling services and providing information. It is a good idea to make your website a source of information on fitness as well as on your business. After all, if a potential client adds your site to their favourite websites then they may well keep coming back to it – which is an excellent way to sell your services.

Within your website you could have the following pages:

- A welcome page – this will include your mission statement, your contact details and what you offer.
- An 'about me/us' page – this will introduce you and your qualifications.
- A feedback/contact page – this should be linked to your email address. Preferably your email address should be info@(your website address), not (name)@email service provider, such as Yahoo or Google. This will look more professional.
- Details of affiliates – these are a source of secondary income. You sign up to be a link to a business through your website. Then every time someone purchases from your affiliate you earn a commission.
- A 'useful links' page – this will provide visitors to your website with a handy resource to revisit.
- Testimonies – previous and current testimonies from your clients. Use real names only if you have explicit permission in writing.

Summary

Once you have started to work in the industry, you can start to use the development of in-house PT client bases to make yourself more marketable and employable. When you are established in-house, you may well be considering taking external clients to supplement your income, or as a basis for moving into self-employment. If you decide to set up your own business, use market research and a business plan to help formulate your ideas and take advantage of professional advice on offer. Remember that nothing comes easy: you will need to work hard and not allow setbacks to stop you from achieving your goals. Learning from your mistakes and persevering will give you the best chance of having a long-term successful business. Good luck!

Further study

The following books are recommended:

DTI (2006) *The no-nonsense guide to starting a business.* Department of Trade and Industry.
Lynn, J (2003) *Start your own personal training business.* Entrepreneur Press.
St Michael, M (2004) *Becoming a personal trainer for dummies.* Wiley Publishing.

Helpful websites include:

www.fitnessmanagement.com/ – a good source of business-related articles on subjects such as retention of PT clients.
www.ptonthenet.com/ – subscription-based resource provider for PTs.
www.workout-uk.co.uk/ – UK fitness industry news.
www.fitpro.com/fitpro/magazines.cfm – UK fitness industry magazine providers.
www.fitnessbusinesspro.com/ – more fitness industry articles are available from this US website.

Job opportunities are advertised on various websites. Try:

www.leisurejobs.co.uk
www.4leisurerecruitment.co.uk
www.redhotcareers.co.uk/vacancies.php

References

ACSM (2002) *Exercise management for persons with chronic diseases and disabilities.* 2nd edition. Human Kinetics.

ACSM (2004) *ACSM's resources for the personal trainer.* Lippincott Williams & Wilkins.

ACSM (2005) *ACSM's guidelines for exercise testing and prescription.* 7th edition. Lippincott Williams & Wilkins.

ACSM (2007) *ACSM's resources for the personal trainer.* 2nd edition. Lippincott Williams & Wilkins.

Baechle, T and Earle, R (2000) *Essentials of strength training and conditioning.* 2nd edition. Human Kinetics.

Baechle, T and Earle, R (2003) *NSCA's essentials of personal training.* Human Kinetics.

Bompa, T (1994) *Theory and methodology of training: the key to athletic performance.* 3rd edition. Kendall Hunt.

Brouns, F (2002) *Essentials of sports nutrition.* 2nd edition. John Wiley & Sons.

Chu, D (1998) *Jumping into plyometrics.* 2nd edition. Human Kinetics.

Chu, D (2003) *Plyometric exercises with the medicine ball.* 2nd edition. Bittersweet Publishing.

Clark, N (2003) *Nancy Clark's sports nutrition guidebook.* 3rd edition. Human Kinetics.

Dick, F (2007) *Sports training principles.* 5th edition. A & C Black.

DTI (2006) *The no-nonsense guide to starting a business.* Department of Trade and Industry.

Fleck, S and Kraemer, W (2003) *Designing resistance training programs.* 3rd edition. Human Kinetics.

Fox, E, Bowers, R and Foss, M (1998) *The physiological basis for exercise and sport.* 2nd edition. McGraw-Hill.

Haase, A (2004) 'Leisure-time physical activity in university students from 23 countries: associations with health beliefs, risk awareness, and national economic development'. *Preventive Medicine* 39: 182–90.

Howley, F (2007) *Fitness professionals handbook.* 5th edition. Human Kinetics.

Lawrence, D (2006) *GP referral schemes, working with referred clients.* A & C Black.

Locke, E and Latham, G (2002) 'Building a practically useful theory of goal setting and task motivation'. *American Psychologist*, 57(9): 705–17.

Lynn, J (2003) *Start your own personal training business.* Entrepreneur Press.

McArdle, W, Katch, F and Katch, V (2005) *Sports and exercise nutrition*. 2nd edition. Lippincott Williams & Wilkins.

McArdle, W, Katch, F and Katch, V (2006) *Exercise physiology: energy, nutrition, and human performance*. 6th edition. Lippincott Williams & Wilkins.

McAtee, R (2007) *Facilitated stretching*. 3rd edition. Human Kinetics.

Maclaren, D (2007) *Nutrition and sport: advances in sport and exercise science*. Churchill Livingston.

Marcus, B and Forsyth, L (2003) *Motivating people to be physically active*. Human Kinetics.

Penedo, F and Dahn, J (2005) 'Exercise and well-being: a review of mental and physical health benefits associated with physical activity'. *Current Opinion in Psychiatry*, 18(2): 189–93.

Power, K, Behm, D, Cahill, F, Carroll, M and Young, W (2004) 'An acute bout of static stretching: effects on force and jumping performance'. *Medicine & Science in Sports & Exercise*, 36(8): 1389–96.

Potvin, A and Jesperson, M (2004) *The great medicine ball handbook*. 3rd edition. Productive Fitness.

St Michael, M (2004) *Becoming a personal trainer for dummies*. Wiley Publishing.

Siff, M (2003) *Supertraining*. 6th edition. Supertraining Institute.

Strecher, V (1995) 'Goal setting as a strategy for health behavior change'. *Health Education & Behavior*, 22 (2): 190–200.

Weinberg, R and Gould, D (2007) *Foundations of sport and exercise psychology*. 4th edition. Human Kinetics.

Wilmore, J and Costill, D (2005) *Physiology of sport and exercise*. 3rd edition. Human Kinetics.

Wolff, R (2002) *Home bodybuilding: three easy steps to building your body and changing your life*. Adams Media Corp.

YMCA (2000) *YMCA fitness testing and assessment manual*. 4th edition. Human Kinetics.

Index